To kyle + diane

all the best

桃の木 MOMO·NO·KI

CHRISTOPHER BURT

First published in Great Britain in 2014 by
www.awaywithmedia.com
Shrewsbury SY3 7LN

© Christopher Burt

ISBN: 978-0-9576292-5-7 (paperback)
      978-0-9576292-6-4 (hardback)

Edited, photographed and published by
Andrew Richardson

For my mother, Valerie; my long-suffering wife, Jo; and my ever-so-patient and ever-so-proud father, Chris

Foreword

By Suree Coates

I first met Chris and his wife, Jo, over a long, raucous supper at my restaurant, The King and Thai. I enjoyed his company enormously. The one thing that struck me most of all was his passion for oriental food.

He was extremely knowledgeable and remarkably enthusiastic. He had learned about myriad flavours during taste adventures in south-east Asia. And he had dazzled countless thousands of customers with tastes that they had never previously tried.

Chris is an instinctive cook. Many of his recipes are stored in his head: or, at least they were, until he decided to write his first book. You won't find Chris telling you to add 5ml of this sauce, or 5g of that spice. He'll encourage you to use his book as a guide, and then season food so that it is suitable to your tastes.

Oriental food is not easy to cook. I should know. I have been cooking Thai cuisine since I was five years old and during the past two years I've been named Britain's Thai Chef of the Year and Britain's Best South East Asian Chef. It requires patience and understanding; it requires a willingness to balance complicated flavours and, above all else, it requires skill.

Chris has all of those qualities in abundance. He understands his need to balance sugar and salt, sweet and sour, umami and bitter. He has an exceptional palate and his knowledge of ingredients is remarkable.

Since meeting Chris, we've learned from one another. Chris has come to my restaurant to spend time in service with me. I've been to his restaurant to learn from him. It's proved a mutually beneficial partnership.

He has many admirable qualities: not least his energy, his enthusiasm and his passion. But I think the thing that has impressed me most is his single-minded determination.

Chris is a Yorkshireman who runs a busy kitchen in landlocked Shropshire. You'd expect him to focus on classic British cuisine. And yet he has followed his heart to cook the food of his dreams. And in doing so, he has educated an entire county in the joys of one of the most remarkable and satisfying cuisines on the planet.

I don't just admire Chris and enjoy his food, I also respect the fact that he's a courageous, trendsetting chef who walks along the road less travelled. I hope you enjoy his recipes, just as I do.

Momo·No·Ki

Momo·No·Ki may well be The Peach Tree's kid brother. But that doesn't mean it will forever be in its shadow.

Momo·No·Ki and The Peach Tree will enhance one another. The symbiosis that I've enjoyed with some of my best suppliers, like Mark and Misako at Setonaikai, or my fishmonger Ian, at Barkworths, is what we intend to achieve with the two restaurants.

They will enhance and complement each other. They will travel in different directions and be led by different teams, but they'll have the same objective: to deliver food that is delicious and puts a smile on our customers' faces.

I'm fortunate that I've had 16 years experience at The Peach Tree. Some of the mistakes that I've made along the way have been invaluable. Whenever something goes wrong, I write it down so that I can learn from it and avoid doing the same thing twice.

In that respect, Momo·No·Ki is lucky. The wisdom of our experiences should enable us to steer it along the right path.

In terms of food and service, Momo·No·Ki will be Asia For Everybody.

The authentic tastes and textures that I've enjoyed so much during my many years of travelling will feature in an eclectic menu that provides the best of all things. Asia has many crowd-pleasing dishes and we'll

be bringing them to bear in our new restaurant.

One of the most valuable lessons I learned in recent times was at the inaugural Shrewsbury Food Festival, in 2013. Huge numbers of people attended and enjoyed the diverse array of food and drink that was on offer.

We viewed the event as an opportunity to try something different. Instead of sticking to a traditional English menu, like many of the hot-food vendors, we took a gamble and served Korean barbecued pork. It flew out of the door. People couldn't get enough.

By the middle of the first afternoon, we'd sold more than we planned to sell during the entire weekend. That convinced me that we were right to explore a broader range of Asian foods. And that's exactly what we intend to do at Momo·No·Ki.

The people of Shropshire – and from far beyond the county boundaries – show their appetite for Asian food day-in, day-out at The Peach Tree. The launch of Momo·No·Ki will give us an even greater opportunity to satisfy that appetite. So pull up a chair: what do you fancy? Ramen, dashi, sashimi, or a plate of our lip-smacking Korean barbecued pork.

Why Momo·No·Ki?

It's a simple enough question. And there's a simple enough answer.

The Japanese translation for Peach Tree is Momo·No·Ki. And our new restaurant, Momo·No·Ki, is our interpretation of the best south-east Asian cuisine. We've created classic dishes – ramens, dashis, Korean pork and the like – to present Asian food for everybody.

My frequent trips to all parts of south-east Asia have provided me with a deep understanding of the tastes, textures and flavours that are everywhere from high-end restaurants to late-night street markets. I've cooked in the Far East and learned from the experts.

Our food is just as edgy, just as delicious and just as intoxicating as the dishes that are served in Bali, Kuala Lumpur, Bangkok, Tokyo, Phnom Penh, Nha Trang, Vientiane and Naypyidaw.

The origins of Momo·No·Ki can be traced back to one of the most important relationships in my life as a chef: I'm great friends with a couple of self-confessed foodies, Mark and Misako, who run Setonaikai, in Shrewsbury. They specialise in authentic ingredients, cookware and tableware from Japan and the Far East.

Mark and Misako are continually bringing in new ingredients which challenge us and enable us to give our customers new, exciting and authentic flavours.

The idea for Momo·No·Ki developed when I fell in love with the cooking of David Chang, the Korean-American chef who created the Momofuku restaurant group.

Chefs including Claude Bosi, Sat Bains, Glynn Purnell and René Redzepi have also influenced my plans. They are ahead of the rest; they show that it can be done. Chefs such as Roy Choi, who was born in the same year as me, have revolutionised the restaurant scene.

Good food has moved away from the foundations of classical French cuisine. Even here in sleepy old Shrewsbury, things are moving forwards.

As a chef, there's never been a more exciting time than now. I've taken inspiration from my own food heroes and created new, pan-Asian tastes. Our menu is truly hybrid.

People don't just want fish and chips – they want a delicious bowl of ramen. They no longer want apple pie and custard – they want crackerjack puddings like Burty's Bassetts. Customers demand two things: food that is delicious and food that makes them smile.

Some of the dishes in this book are enormously complicated. We've avoided the easy route and pushed ourselves harder and harder each week. We're glad that we have. Our food is getting better and better.

The kitchens at The Peach Tree and Momo·No·Ki thrive on creativity. I don't want to be remembered as a chef who did it for the money – I'm a chef who does it for the kicks.

桃の木

Contents

桃の木

MOMO·NO·KI

RAMEN

Rules of ramen

Few foods are as satisfying as ramen. The popular noodle dishes are widespread in Japan. A typical ramen dish will feature boiled noodles served in a flavoured dashi, with various toppings.

We're one of a small number of restaurants to make our own ramen – ramen noodles contain an alkaline solution called kansui, which is notoriously difficult to get hold of in the UK. Consequently, very few people make them.

The alkaline solution is essential to the preparation of good ramen. Without kansui, the noodles would start to disintegrate in the hot dashi, which would continue to cook them. The effect would be the same as leaving pasta in a hot soup, they would simply break up. The kansui prevents that process.

The godfather of ramen is Momofuku Ando, who died in 2007 aged 96. He invented the world's first instant noodle product, chicken ramen. He was ahead of his time, inventing the product in 1958. In 1971, he created another new product, Cup Noodle, the world's first cup-type noodle product. Momofuku became known as Mr Noodles and is credited with helping to feed a war-ravaged Japan on a budget, which allowed the country to get back on its feet.

Ramen chefs train for a long time to make good ramen soup. Typical flavourings might include chicken bones, pork bones, kombu and vegetables such as ginger, negi onion, garlic and mushrooms. Ramen toppings typically include negi, seasoned bamboo shoots, fishcakes – kamaboko or narutomaki – beansprouts, spring onions, pickled Korean or Japanese daikon, cavalo nero or winter kales, sweetcorn, sesame seeds, chilli shrimp oil, kimchi, and 62-degree duck egg.

RAMEN
800g STRONG WHITE FLOUR
300g TEPID WATER
2 tsp KANSUI
50g FINE CORNMEAL

First, make your kansui, by heating baking powder in between an exopat non-stick, heatproof mat at 150C for an hour.

Now, combine all of your ingredients and knead for 10 minutes. Wrap your ramen in clingfilm and allow to rest for 35 minutes in the fridge.

Cut the ramen into sections and roll out the dough. Roll it through a pasta machine, using a spaghetti attachment. Now put into 200g bundles on a wooden board.

To serve. Blanch the ramen in water on a rolling boil for two minutes, until ready.

Serve with dashi and your chosen toppings.

The dashi commandments

If there's one technique that you really have to master it's learning how to make dashi. Dashi is Japanese stock, which is the base for soups, dipping sauces and simmered dishes, which are called nimono.

It can be made with a variety of ingredients, including kombu (dried kelp), katsuobushi (dried, fermented, smoked bonito), niboshi (dried sardines), shiitake mushrooms and more besides. Dashi is at its best on the day it's made, though it can be stored in the fridge for a couple of days. Instant dashi powder is available, but that frequently contains MSG so I'd recommend you learn how to make it. Good dashi makes your dishes taste so much better.

It is remarkably simple to make, though you'll find you'll improve over time as you become more practised in the art. It is, for instance, far easier to make a good dashi than a good chicken or beef stock.

I've listed 10 dashi commandments below, with two other notables. Further recipes and methods follow.

1 water, kombu, shiitake and tomatoes
2 as above, with chicken powder and katsuobushi
3 as dashi number 1, with miso
4 as dashi number 2, with XO sauce
5 as dashi number 1, with black miso
6 as dashi number 2, with tare
7 as dashi number 4, with yuzu pith
8 as dashi number 1, with sesame oil
9 as dashi number 1, with goma shio (sea salt and sesame)
10 as either dashi number 1 or 2, with five- or seven-spice

Notable others

11 as dashi number 4, with chilli shrimp oil
12 as dashi number 1 or 2, with a vegetable purée – carrot or beetroot, perhaps

TRADITIONAL DASHI
2 sheets KOMBU
2 ltrs WATER
KATSUOBUSHI, to taste

Add the kombu and water to a pan, put it onto a medium simmer, then turn the heat off and let it steep for 15 minutes. Add the katsuobushi. Use straight away, or refrigerate. It's that simple.

MOMO•NO•KI DASHI – SHOYU DASHI
2 sheets KOMBU
2 ltrs WATER
10 BEEF TOMATOES
500g SHIITAKE
2 tbsp LIGHT SOY

Follow the same method as the traditional dashi, but adding the tomatoes and shiitake to the pot of water and simmering for an additional 20 minutes.

Momo•No•Ki bacon dashi. This is the same as the Momo•No•Ki dashi, above, but add 500g of smoked bacon bits and simmer for an extra 30 minutes.

MOMO•NO•KI RAMEN BROTH – TONKOTSU
3 pieces KOMBU
8 ltrs WATER
2kg CHICKEN BONES
2kg PORK BONES, split
500g SMOKED BACON BITS
2 bunches SPRING ONIONS
2 SPANISH or WHITE ONIONS
6 large CARROTS
10 BEEF TOMATOES
200g SHIITAKE
SOY SAUCE to taste

Preheat the oven to 180C and roast the pork and chicken bones for 40 minutes. Start as with the bacon dashi recipe, then add the bones and simmer for six to eight hours. Add the spring onion, carrot and onion and simmer for a further 45 minutes. Then strain through muslin and finish with soy or tare.

Variations. You can vary your dashis by adding the following, to season: tare, soy, XO sauce, yuzu pith, chilli shrimp oil, sesame seeds or oil, miso, oyster sauce and others.

Tare is chicken-infused soy sauce, which I mention in several recipes

TARE
2kg CHICKEN BONES
300ml SAKE
300ml MIRIN
400ml LIGHT SOY
WHITE PEPPER
200ml WATER

Roast or sauté the chicken bones until they are golden. Add all ingredients to a pan and simmer on a medium heat for 10 minutes. Reduce further, if necessary. Strain and use straight away, or refrigerate for up to three days.

18

MOMO·NO·KI

Momo·No·Ki Ramen

This is our signature ramen and it's a real crowd-pleaser. It features everything that's great about ramen: deliciously light dashi, fresh ramen noodles, a fudgy sous vide duck egg, slices of southern fried pork and other incredible flavours and textures. It's a nailed-on classic that's fast become one of our best sellers.

FOR ONE LARGE SERVING
400ml SHOYU DASHI (p16)
¾ tbsp XO SAUCE
150g RAMEN NOODLES (p14)
Small handful FINELY CUT SPRING
   ONIONS to garnish
2 tbsp HOMEMADE KIMCHI (p32)
2 slices KAMABOKO FISH CAKE
2 slices KOREAN PICKLED DAIKON
2 slices SOUTHERN FRIED TOGARASHI
   PORK BELLY (p102)
½ SOUS VIDE DUCK EGG (p49)
100ml TEMPURA BATTER (p49)
4 tbsp POLENTA CRUMBS
1 tbsp TOGARASHI SPICE
Small handful BEANSPROUTS

OPTIONAL EXTRAS
CHILLI SHRIMP OIL
CHICKEN-INFUSED SOY SAUCE

The dish is fairly simple to assemble, once you've obtained all of the separate components.

Start with your dashi. Take your shoyu dashi and add a splash of XO sauce to it. XO sauce is a spicy seafood sauce that you'll find at most Asian supermarkets. It includes dried scallops, chilli peppers, dried shrimp, garlic and other ingredients. I tend to add about three quarters of a tbsp per person, based on a large serving with 400ml of dashi. However, it is up to you to season to taste. Some will like more, others will prefer less.

Take two slices of pre-cooked pork belly, approximately 1cm by 4cm. Dip into a light tempura batter. Now roll it in a bowl, filled with a well-mixed blend of polenta and togarashi spice. Put both pieces into a hot fryer, at around 170C, and cook for three minutes. Remove and strain.

Blanch your noodles and set aside.

Assembly. Warm your ramen bowl, then warm your shoyu XO dashi and pour in. Add your pre-blanched noodles, half a sous vide duck egg, kamaboko fish cake, Korean pickled daikon, homemade kimchi and a small handful of beansprouts. You can further season with a chicken-infused soy sauce, or chilli shrimp oil. Chilli shrimp oil is the go-to ingredient because it will give your dish more bite. Add two slices of southern fried togarashi pork belly. Garnish with finely cut spring onions.

Taishoken Ramen

You'll never have eaten a surf and turf quite like this one. The sweet-salty scallop and savoury pork are enhanced by southern fried togarashi spice. It's a melt-in-the-mouth dish.

FOR ONE LARGE SERVING
400ml MOMO·NO·KI RAMEN BROTH (p17)
150g RAMEN NOODLES (p14)
1 tbsp KATSUOBUSHI
1 tbsp CHICKEN-INFUSED SOY SAUCE
2 tbsp HOMEMADE KIMCHI (p32)
Small handful BEANSPROUTS
ASIAN GREENS, SUCH AS PAK CHOI OR
  BOK CHOI
½ SOUS VIDE DUCK EGG (p49)
1 slice CONFIT PORK SHOULDER (p103)
1 or 2 HAND-DIVED SCALLOPS
4 tbsp TEMPURA BATTER (p49)
4 tbsp POLENTA
1 tbsp TOGARASHI SPICE

OPTIONAL EXTRAS
CHICKEN-INFUSED SOY SAUCE
CHILLI SHRIMP OIL
Extra KATSUOBUSHI

We're using a salt-and-pepper-based dashi. Warm through and finish by adding a tbsp of katsuobushi. Allow that to infuse, then strain. Add in a tbsp of chicken-infused soy sauce, to season.

Blanch four or five pieces of Asian greens, such as pak choi or bok choi, for 60–90 seconds. If you can't get those, use kale or cavolo nero.

Slice a medium-thickness piece of confit pork shoulder, which has been cooked in a star anise-infused oil and allowed to cool. Thinner pieces are more easily warmed by the dashi.

Take a scallop, discarding any roe, and cut in half. Then dip into the tempura batter before rolling through a well-mixed bowl of polenta and togarashi spice. Deep-fry at 170C for 120 seconds, until golden brown. Remove and drain. Blanch your ramen noodles.

Assembly. We take a warm bowl and add our dashi, pre-blanched ramen noodles, two tbsp of homemade kimchi and a small handful of beansprouts. Add the pork shoulder and halved duck egg and then place the togarashi scallops on top. Sprinkle liberally with spring onions and further season, if required, with additional chicken-infused soy sauce or chilli shrimp oil. You can offer further katsuobushi on the side, if you like.

Misako Ramen

A delicate balance of citrus, salty seaweed and deliciously fresh, five-spiced prawns give this ramen a real wow factor. The combination of textures and tastes is intoxicating.

FOR 1 LARGE SERVING
400ml MOMO·NO·KI SHOYU BROTH (p16)
150g RAMEN NOODLES (p14)
½ tsp YUZU, INCLUDING JUICE AND ZEST
½ tsp XO SAUCE
5 LARGE PRAWNS
4 tbsp TEMPURA BATTER (p49)
1 tsp FIVE SPICE
1 tbsp KIMCHI (p32)
Small handful BEANSPROUTS
2 slices KAMOBOKO FISH CAKE
2 slices PICKLED DAIKON
½ 62-DEGREE SOUS VIDE DUCK EGG (P49)
1 sheet NORI
FINELY CHOPPED SPRING ONIONS

OPTIONAL EXTRAS
CHILLI SHRIMP OIL or SESAME OIL

Infuse your normal dashi with yuzu, which gives it a wonderfully light, zesty flavour and is available at most Asian supermarkets. Now add ½ tsp of XO sauce and gently simmer, without allowing to boil. Clean, de-head and de-vein your large prawns, so that only the tip of the tail is left on them. Dip into tempura batter, holding by the tail, then roll in a five-spiced polenta mix. Deep fry at 170C for around two minutes, until golden. You can use nori seaweed, which is relatively easy to handle and does not require pre-soaking. Blanch your ramen noodles.

Assembly. Take the sheet of seaweed and fold into a pyramid shape. Place on the side of the dish. Add the dashi, noodles, kimchi, beansprouts, kamoboko fish cake, pickled daikon and sous vide duck egg. Arrange the deep-fried prawns to the side and season with a little chilli shrimp oil or sesame oil. Sprinkle liberally with spring onions.

MOMO·NO·KI

Bo Ssam Ramen

The blend of spice, citrus and sumptuous, five-spiced confit duck in this dish is intoxicating. The addition of greens and pickles balances out the dish, making it deliciously satisfying. "Bo ssam" means wrapped, in Korean.

400ml MOMO·NO·KI RAMEN BROTH (p17)
KATSUOBUSHI
CHICKEN-INFUSED SOY SAUCE
4 ASIAN-SPICED CONFIT DUCK LEGS
  (p103)
150g RAMEN NOODLES (p14)
Couple of leaves CAVOLO NERO
Small handful BEANSPROUTS
2 slices KAMOBOKO FISH CAKE
2 slices PICKLED DAIKON
½ A 62-DEGREE SOUS VIDE DUCK EGG
  (p49)
Slices of KYURI (PICKLED JAPANESE
  CUCUMBER)
YUZU PEEL

OPTIONAL EXTRAS
SESAME SEEDS, CHILLI SHRIMP OIL,
  SESAME OIL OR CHICKEN-INFUSED SOY
  SAUCE

We shred the meat from our four cooled confit duck legs and set aside. Now we prepare our shoyu dashi, which is a sea-salt dashi, by infusing it with katsuobushi. Once the flavours have infused, strain and discard the residual katsuobushi. Simmer, without boiling, and add chicken-infused soy sauce to season. Blanch the long black Italian cabbage and set aside. Blanch your ramen noodles.

Assembly. Add the dashi to a warm bowl. Season the duck with sea salt or chicken-infused soy sauce. Wrap it in the cavalo nero. Add the ramen, bean sprouts, kamaboko fish cake, pickled daikon and kyuri asazuke, which is available at most Asian supermarkets. Add half a 62-degree duck egg. Add our wrapped duck. Sprinkle yuzu peel on the top of the bo ssam. Add other garnishes and condiments to suit, such as sesame seeds, chilli shrimp oil, sesame oil or chicken-infused soy sauce.

Kangaroodon

Kangaroo is a delicious meat that has a similar taste to venison and buffalo. It's widely available in Australia, though you'll need to buy it from a specialist supplier here in the UK. It's nutritious and low in fat – and this flavoursome dish showcases it at its best.

FOR 1 LARGE SERVING
400ml MOMO·NO·KI RAMEN BROTH (p17)
150g UDON NOODLES – or a portion-sized
  packet from the supermarket (p14)
150g KANGAROO LOIN – or other lean cut
TOGARASHI SEVEN-SPICE POWDER
WINTER GREENS, or CAVOLO NERO
Small handful FINELY CUT SPRING
  ONIONS to garnish
½ SOUS VIDE DUCK EGG (p49)
Small handful BEANSPROUTS
SEAWEED – WAKAME

OPTIONAL EXTRAS
CHILLI SHRIMP OIL

We take a 150g piece of kangaroo and lightly oil it with rapeseed oil. We sprinkle over togarashi Japanese seven spice and then we leave it to infuse. Blanch the winter greens, or cavolo nero. If you prefer, you can use the leaves of a hard green cabbage. I prefer wakame seaweed for this dish, which needs to be reconstituted, though some home cooks may prefer nero. Blanch your udon noodles.

Now, cook off your kangaroo. Season it with a 50:50 mixture of rapeseed oil and sesame seed oil for 2–2½ minutes on either side. Now take it out of the pan and rest for eight or nine minutes.

Assembly. Take a warm bowl and add your warm dashi, blanched udon noodles and winter greens. Add half a 62-degree duck egg and reconstituted wakame seaweed. To finish the dish we add our kangaroo and slice it very carefully. If your kangaroo shows signs of leaching any further juices, leave it for a further minute, before adding to the bowl. Sprinkle with spring onions and chilli shrimp oil.

The 3am

You'll guess how this dish came about. I spent most of the early hours of the morning buzzing after a busy service, devising new recipes or catching up on work from the previous day. This dish gives me a hit of satisfying flavour in the wee small hours – and it's just about perfect at all other times of day. This comes in a smaller portion size compared to the other ramens. It's great after a few cheeky beers.

FOR 1 LARGE SERVING
200–300ml MOMO·NO·KI RAMEN BROTH
   (p17 – infuse with bacon to give a smokier
   flavour)
150g RICE NOODLES (p14)
2 slices BELLY PORK (p102)
2 tbsp KIMCHI (p32)
Small handful BEANSPROUTS
Sprinkling of SESAME SEEDS
Handful FINELY CHOPPED SPRING
   ONIONS
2 tbsp BULGOGI SAUCE
½ SOUS VIDE DUCK EGG (p49)

Blanch your rice noodles. Now cut your belly pork into pieces that are around 3cm thick, leaving the crackling on. Pop that into a fryer for three minutes, then set to one side to rest. Then it's simply a question of assembling your ingredients.

Assembly. Pour a little bulgogi sauce into your warmed bowl. It usually goes with beef, but it also works really well with pork. Then sprinkle seasame seeds and spring onions onto it and give it a good swish, so that it's evenly coated. Now add the rice noodles, kimchi, beansprouts, and halved duck egg and pour in your smoked bacon dashi, until it's three-quarters full. Enjoy.

桃の木

SIDES

Apple Kimchi Salad

Kimchi is a traditional Korean side dish made from vegetables and a variety of seasonings. It is fermented, which helps to give it its unique flavour. In Korea, people prepare kimchi by fermenting vegetables underground in jars for several months; my version allows you to make it much more quickly. Kimchi is Korea's national dish and can be made from radish, cucumber, scallion, cabbage or a variety of other ingredients.

KIMCHI
1 ASIAN CABBAGE
SALT
KOREAN RED BEAN PASTE
1 tbsp SWEET CHILLI
4 tbsp BULGOGI SAUCE
1 tbsp DRIED CHILLI FLAKES

APPLE KIMCHI SALAD
1 GRANNY SMITH APPLE
½ tbsp KIMCHI
1tbsp SESAME SEEDS
1 tbsp BULGOGI SAUCE

Kimchi. Cut your Asian cabbage in half, then in half again. Continue to do so, until you have small pieces that are around 2cm × 2cm. Salt the pieces liberally and leave to drain, until the water stops running out. Now wash off the salt and set aside. Make your fermentation liquid by taking a small pot of Korean red bean paste. Spoon a quarter of a pot over the cabbage, then the sweet chilli, bulgogi and dried chilli flakes. Mix that together thoroughly with the cabbage.

There are different ways to ferment it. You can put it in a pot with cling film sealing it, pop it in the fridge and leave it for up to three days. Or you can achieve the same results more rapidly by leaving your container at room temperature. Remember to take the clingfilm off every now and then, to allow gases to escape.

Apple Kimchi Salad: assembly. Slice your apple finely on a mandolin. Make a stack from four pieces, placing kimchi between each. Skewer to hold together, drizzle with bulgogi sauce and finish with sesame seeds.

Edamame Hummus/Tempura Greens

These dishes are accompaniments, or components of other dishes. You can serve them as appetisers or along with mains. These are the basic recipes, which you can scale up or scale down as you require.

EDAMAME HUMMUS
400g EDAMAME BEANS
1 BIRD'S-EYE CHILLI
3 tbsp SESAME OIL
1 tbsp LIGHT SOY SAUCE
20g PEELED AND DICED GINGER
5g BLACK SESAME SEEDS
3 GARLIC CLOVES, pulped
1 tbsp THAI FISH SAUCE
Handful of CHOPPED CORIANDER
WATER, as required

TEMPURA GREENS
10 CAVOLO NERO LEAVES
200g PLAIN FLOUR
200g CORNFLOUR
SODA WATER – around 500ml, enough to
   make a batter which coats your finger
SALT and PEPPER
CRUSHED ICE

Edamame Hummus. Blend the ingredients together in a food processor for two to three minutes, adding water gradually, to achieve the desired consistency. Continue to check and adjust the seasoning.

Tempura Greens. Mix together 90 per cent of your plain flour with the cornflour and salt and pepper. Now add soda water and ice, to make a slightly viscous solution. Once the ice has melted, combine further until you have your batter. You want to achieve a state in which the batter coats your finger, so it's neither too thick or too runny.

Now coat your cavolo nero in the flour, then dip it into the tempura batter. Fry straight away at 190C for two minutes, turning twice, until golden brown.

MOMO·NO·KI

桃の木

Piggy Bits/Noci

These delicious, deep-fried cubes of pork with a bulgogi sauce are ridiculously moreish. We have customers who come back time and time again just to order a pot – we dare not take them off the menu. Noci are the perfect appetisers. Packed with protein, brimful of flavour and designed to get your tastebuds tingling, the only trouble is our customers end up eating too many.

PIGGY BITS
200g CONFIT BELLY PORK
2 tbsp BULGOGI SAUCE
1 tsp BLACK SESAME SEEDS, toasted

OPTIONAL EXTRAS
CHILLI SHRIMP OIL

NOCI
A mix of NUTS AND SEEDS, including
    walnuts, pistachios, pumpkin seeds,
    sunflower seeds, peanuts, almonds,
    linseeds and hemp seeds
1 tbsp SWEET CHILLI
ROSEMARY
Generous pinch of SALT
1 tbsp SESAME OIL
1 tbsp RAPESEED OIL

Piggy Bits. Cut your confit belly pork into 1cm strips and deep fry for two minutes at 180C. Toss liberally in bulgogi sauce and sprinkle with toasted sesame seeds. If you want to turn up the heat, season with additional chilli shrimp oil.

Noci. Heat a dry pan and add all ingredients. Pan fry for about 90 seconds, until golden brown. Serve.

37

SIDES

桃の木

MOMO·NO·KI

SUSHI AND SASHIMI

NISHIKI

最高級特撰米
NISHIKI
BRAND

NET WT. 2.5 Kg / NETTO: 2.5 kg / POIDS NET. 2.5 kg
Peso netto 2.5 kg / Cont. Net. 2.5 kg / NETTO: 2.5 kg
Nettovikt 2.5 kg / Nette vægt: 2.5 Kg / BEC HETTO 2.5 КГ

Rules of sushi and sashimi

There are two immovable rules for great sushi and sashimi: **1** It must be fresh; **2** Keep it simple.

Providing you never waver from those rules, you'll be fine. If ever you feel the temptation to overcomplicate, remember this: the point of fresh sashimi is to deliver the purest form of delicious ocean cuisine to the plate.

Ingredients. The world's your oyster – and your lobster, and your abalone, and your ebi fried shrimp. Nothing's off limits . . . well, almost nothing. Try gobo rolls and futomaki rolls, and use vegetables such as avocado and cucumber. Mango makes a wonderful addition, while sea urchin, king fish, tuna, flying fish, sea bream, octopus, scallop and other molluscs are all delicious.

Garnishes. There are additions that enhance the flavours of sushi and sashimi. Garnishes such as daikon, pink pickled ginger, a dab of horseradish-ey wasabi paste and umami-laden soy sauce all help. Caviars add delicious flavour, texture and colour.

Presentation and trimming. A small number of chefs will insist that you must make sushi or sashimi to a particular size or shape. That's nonsense. The most important thing is to trim your dishes so that you present the finest quality possible. Remove all sinew or fat and make sure you present only the freshest, most tender fish.

Essential tools. If you're making sashimi and sushi, you'll need a few essential kitchen tools. A bamboo rolling mat and high-quality knife are necessary, as are vegetable peelers and tweezers. You won't need much more than that. Sushi and sashimi are not expensive to make and, unlike many other dishes, don't cost a fortune to make.

And finally . . . I've said it elsewhere and I'll say it again here: forge a relationship with your fishmonger. Sushi and sashimi are all about celebrating the freshest and most vibrant ingredients available. So talk to your supplier. Ask about dayboat fish that were delivered with 24 hours and have not been frozen. You only want the best, so ask the experts.

shimi Plate

high-quality Japanese sashimi knife is essential. If used
 it will elevate your skills to a new level. Make sure you cut your
 to the same thickness, so that it is uniform.

aking cuts, place your fish loin or seafood on a board, wet your
knife and slice diagonally across the piece of fish. Make sure
against the grain and slice downwards and to the left.

ake your cuts with one sturdy motion, using the entire length of
. Avoid making sawing movements, which damage the fish.
can be sliced so that it is almost paper-thin. You are giving
sts a taste, rather than a mouthful of protein. Sushi slices can
r.

ish such as tuna, halibut and sea bass is one skill, but you
lso learn how to butterfly. This helps you to open up food, such
s.

e, before arriving at the final stages, you will need to have
 filleted and boned your fish. To skin your fish, lay the fillet on a
sert the knife between the fillet and the skin and slowly move

the knife back and forward. Deboning techniques vary, depending on
whether you are working with a flat fish or a round fish.

Another important tip is to be patient, particularly if you are new to the
art.

Taking a whole fish, removing the fillets and then slicing paper-thin
pieces of sashimi is a technique that requires patience and practice. So
don't worry if it takes time to get it right.

My selection of sashimi includes whatever is available from my
fishmonger on a particular day; it changes constantly.

I might feature tuna, king fish, salmon, sea bass, scallop and halibut.
You can control your garnishes more easily, by selecting jars of caviar
as well as pickled ginger, soy and wasabi.

FOR THE RICE
400g SUSHI RICE
450ml WATER
1 sheet DRIED KOMBU, 10cm × 10cr

FOR THE VINEGAR MIX
5 tbsp JAPANESE RICE VINEGAR
2 tbsp SUGAR
2 tbsp MIRIN
½ tbsp SALT

FOR THE FILLING
150g SASHIMI-GRADE TUNA
100g SALMON filleted, pin-boned an
  skinned

FOR THE TOPPINGS
1 tbsp GREEN TOBBIKO
1 tbsp ORANGE TOBBIKO
1 tbsp YELLOW KETA
1 tbsp GOMO WAKAME
EDIBLE FLOWERS
MICRO-AMARYNTH
MICRO-CORIANDER
BLACK SESAME SEEDS

FOR THE SUSHI ROLLS
3 sheets NORI SEAWEED
1 CUCUMBER, cut into batons

FOR THE SIDE
WASABI
SHAVED PINK GINGER
SOY

Sushi Bento Box

Wash the sushi rice until the water is clear, drain and leave to stand for 30 minutes. Put the rice, water and kombu into a rice cooker, and steam until cooked.

For the vinegar mix, boil together the rice vinegar, sugar, mirin and salt in a pan until the sugar dissolves, then allow to cool. Transfer the rice to a Japanese wooden tub (Hangiri) or bowl, and pour a little of the vinegar mix over the top.

Spread the rice evenly, pouring the rest of the vinegar mixture onto it.

Use a slicing action to coat the rice. Fan the rice with a large spatula until it is glossy and has cooled to room temperature.

To make the cucumber maki sushi roll, place the nori sheet on a bamboo sushi mat. Put a good handful of the rice in the middle of the nori, using your fingers to spread an even layer of rice to the edges of the nori.

Pick up the mat, turn it over and lay the cucumber, wasabi and pink ginger along the centre of the nori. Lift up the near edge of the mat, holding the filling in place with your fingers, then gently squeeze along the length of the roll to mould together, lift up the front edge of the mat and push the roll forward to join two edges of the nori.

Cut the sushi roll into six even-sized pieces, and set aside.

To make the futomaki sushi roll, place the nori seaweed sheet on a bamboo sushi mat. Put a good handful of rice in the middle of the nori, using your fingers to spread an even layer of rice to the edges of the nori. Pick up the mat, turn it over and lay the the cut tuna and salmon, wasabi and pink ginger along the centre of the nori.

Turn this upside down on a sheet of clingfilm and, rolling backwards this time, gently squeeze along the length of the roll to mould together, then lift up the front edge of the mat and push the roll forward to join two edges of the nori. Roll in black sesame seeds

Cut the futomaki roll into six even-sized pieces, then top with a comination of toppings – time to get arty.

Put all together in your bento box and serve with wasabi, pink ginger and soy.

桃の木

MOMO·NO·KI

EGGS AND RICE

MOMO·NO·KI

Rules of eggs, rice and vegetables

We're lucky to have a steady of supply of duck eggs and large chicken eggs from our own birds. They are rich and deliciously creamy. Cooking the eggs is an art in itself and, like many modern chefs, we favour the sous-vide method. Sous vide involves cooking food slowly in a low-temperature bath inside vacuum-sealed bags. The water is circulated to ensure even cooking. For eggs, no vacuum-sealed bags are required – they go straight into the water bath.

Basic sous-vide machines are available for as little as £120. We cook our eggs to 62C, which gives soft whites and a fudge-like yolk; 63C will give medium-set whites; 64C will give firm-set whites. It is difficult to recreate the same effect by boiling an egg conventionally, in a pan of water. However, if that's the only option available to you, don't fear. Boil eggs to a semi-soft consistency, remembering that they will continue to cook if placed in warm liquid, like dashi. The duration of cooking will depend on the size of your egg, so it's impossible to give accurate times. Take four-and-a-half minutes as a guide for a normal-sized egg that you're looking to soft boil].

Rice. Not all rice is equal. And not all rice is cooked the same way. Short-grain Japanese rice is very different from basmati, for instance, or arborio rice. Achieving great results each time takes patience

it steams, recognising the bubbling sound of the rice as it reaches a boil, and the crackling hiss when it's almost done. We wash our rice three times before steaming it. The ratio of rice to water will vary according to the type of rice you use, and the equipment you are using. Refer to the instructions to achieve the best results.

Vegetables. Let's cut to the chase on this one. Seasonal, fresh or, better still, homegrown. Just because we're cooking a Japanese dish, or a Korean classic, doesn't mean we can't use British asparagus or French beans. The rules are simple: as with fish, freshest is best. Cook gently, to preserve the flavour and textures of your vegetables. And don't be afraid to experiment: deep-fried herbs might sound strange, but few things are as enjoyable as a basil crisp or a deep-fried sage leaf.

A basic tempura. I've included a basic tempura recipe on page 35, which explains how to cook tempura vegetables. Tempura is almost as popular as sushi and sashimi. Using iced water for the batter is recommended, as that makes the tempura crisper. Preparing the batter immediately before frying is the best option – there is no need to let it rest. Remember to make sauces to go with it. My recipes will give you plenty of suggestions, or try equal parts soy and mirin, with a bit of grated horseradish.

桃の木

Tiger Bowl

Nobody in Japan really makes sushi at home. But it's harder to get good sushi here in the UK, so it's important to have a standby recipe for all occasions. I've suggested a few ingredients here that work well together, but I'm not going to be too prescriptive. You can adjust the dish to suit your own tastes, or to reflect what's available.

VINEGARED RICE (p44)
SASHIMI GRADE FISH, whatever is available
KAMABOKO FISH CAKE
SAMPHIRE
PRESERVED KOMBU
Assorted ingredients from your Asian
 supermarket, including EDIBLE FLOWERS,
 MICROHERBS and SEA HERBS such as
 ICE LETTUCE or SEA BUCKTHORN

Take some vinegared rice, which we use to half fill a wooden box. The box will help to absorb any excess moisture.

Now be a little creative and fill the top half with a range of ingredients, including fish from your sashimi plate, kamaboko fish cake, samphire, preserved kombu and a range of edible flowers, microherbs and sea herbs. Really it's up to you. This is a very, very simple way of eating sushi.

Blanched vegetables such as asparagus and French beans also work well. If using samphire wash it to remove any excess salt.

Okonomiyaki

Is it a bird? Is it a plane? No, it's Okonomiyaki! There are unlimited okonomiyaki recipes in Japan and the dish is particularly popular in Kansai and Hiroshima. 'Okonomi' means 'what you like'; 'yaki' means 'grilled'. It is, therefore, a savoury Japanese pancake featuring whatever you like.

3 DUCK EGGS, (or LARGE HEN'S EGGS)
½ tsp DASHI POWDER
30g PRAWNS
1 SPRING ONION, sliced
30g SOBA NOODLES, blanched
PICKLED DAIKON
Handful of EDAMAME BEANS
Dash of LIGHT SOY SAUCE
¼ of a normal kitchen ladle of DASHI
TONKATSU SAUCE
JAPANESE MAYONNAISE
NORI SEAWEED

The key to a great okonomiyaki is preparation. Put a saucepan on a medium heat first, so that you're ready to cook.

Now take your eggs and whisk with dashi powder. Add in your prawns and your spring onions, as well as your blanched soba noodles and pickled daikon, and pre-popped edamame beans. Add light soy sauce and dashi into the mix. Whisk.

Then pop a sheet of nori under the grill and toast it. You need to be very, very careful that this doesn't catch fire; you need to be very, very quick. Let it cool, then slice it into julienne slices and set aside, along with additional daikon, which can be used as a garnish.

Add the ingredients to your pan and start to cook. I like to start it on the stove, turn it a bit, like a normal omelette. I like to finish under the grill, which gives you a much nicer glaze on the top. It takes three minutes to cook on the base, then 1½–2 minutes under the grill. Take the pan out.

Assembly. I like to serve it in the pan, which gives it an extra wow factor. I use a shop-bought okonomiyaki sauce, or tonkatsu, which is a type of Japanese barbecue condiment. Just give it a liberal drizzle, then sprinkle the top with nori seaweed, pickled daikon and Japanese mayonnaise, which is very different to the French or British varieties.

桃の木

MOMO·NO·KI

VEGETABLES

The Plantation

This is a sensational vegetarian dish that really shows off the freshest, most flavoursome vegetables to their best. It's a subjective dish, it's all about cooking what you like and what's in season. The dashi and miso give it a good dose of umami.

A selection of vegetables, including
  ASPARAGUS, CHANTENAY CARROTS,
  BABY PARSNIPS, SPRING ONIONS,
  CABBAGES, WILD MUSHROOMS (such as
  SHIMEJI and ENOKI) and a few HERITAGE
  TOMATOES
MICROHERBS and EDIBLE FLOWERS
  to garnish

FOR THE DRESSING
2 tbsp BLONDE MISO
1 tbsp YUZU JUICE and PIECES OF PITH
A sprinkling of DRIED CHILLI
A dash of SOY SAUCE
1 tsp RICE WINE VINEGAR
1 tsp MIRIN
Little squeeze of SESAME OIL

Preparing The Plantation can be quite complicated because every single element is cooked differently. The bases of the vegetables are also cut at 90 degrees, so that they're flat and stand upright on the plate and look like . . . well, a plantation. The key to this dish is to give you an idea – there's no need to follow what I've done, just use it as a guide.

In this case, we took small heritage tomatoes, grilled them and popped them to one side to stay warm. We deep-fried our mushrooms until they were nice and crispy, which added extra texture. Then we took asparagus and spring onions, gave them a liberal coating of rapeseed oil and chargrilled them until they were semisoft and the spring onions started to wilt.

The Chantenay carrots were poached in dashi, as were the parsnips. I also deep-fried kale, to add a little crisp texture, before seasoning with sea salt.

For the dressing, simply combine the ingredients, whisk and adjust seasoning.

Assembly. Arrange the dish on a plate and be as rustic as you wish. It's a warm, inviting dish that vegetarians adore. Feel free to be creative. Ingredients like full-size heritage tomatoes and anja potatoes give a good texture. You should drizzle the dressing over, without flooding the plate. The dressing will give it a good umami-feel. Garnish with microcress or rose petals, whatever's in season: microcoriander and amaranth are great.

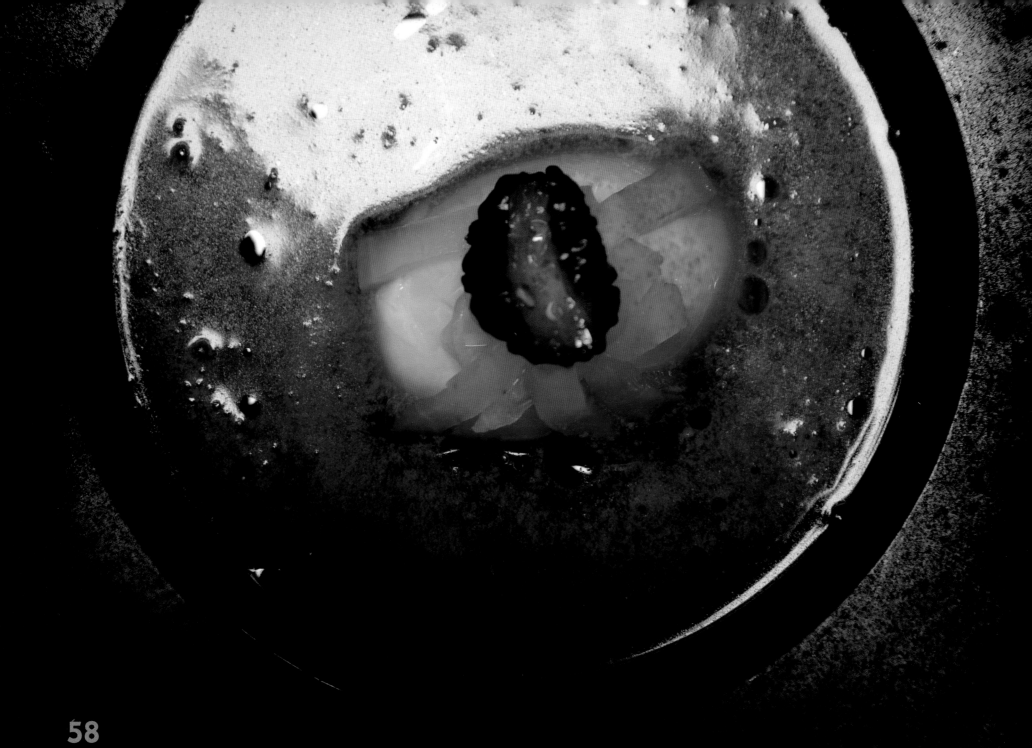

'Beatroots'

This is one of the most colourful dishes on the menu. I'm a huge fan of beetroot, I love the combination of sweet and earthy flavours – and this presentation looks simply stunning. This is a recipe that we make in bulk, though you can easily scale it down.

SERVES 8

2 BEETROOTS
2 sheets KOMBU
2 large TOMATOES
500g DRIED CEPS
2 ltrs WATER
1 DAIKON
SHIBAZUKE
SMOKED SESAME OIL
BEETROOT POWDER
4 DUCK EGGS

First you need to sous vide the 62-degree duck eggs for an hour, then refresh in iced water. Now make your dashi by boiling the beetroots, skin on, until tender, then peeling the skins off and puréeing in a food processor until smooth. In a separate pan, add the kombu, ceps, water and tomatoes and simmer for 30 minutes, without boiling. Take off the heat and add the beetroot purée, mixing thoroughly. Once mixed pass the dashi through a fine tamis.

Assembly. Heat the dashi to no more than 60C – if you boil it, you'll ruin it and it'll taste like a fisherman's welly. Place the egg in the bottom of a bowl and pour the dashi over; this will warm the egg. Julienne the daikon and place on top of the egg. Drizzle with the sesame oil and dust the bowl with beetroot powder (which we buy from MSK, but which you could make by desiccating a beetroot in a very low oven). Garnish with shibazuke, which is a bright purple speciality pickle made from cucumber, eggplant, perilla leaves, ginger and myoga. It has a salty, slightly sour taste and is popular with Kyoto cuisine.

The Garden

We eat with our eyes, as well as our mouths. And this is a dish that thrills all of the senses. It is a visual feast and the flavours are exquisite. Savoury, earthy 'black pudding soil', a Jerusalem artichoke veloute and delicious fresh vegetables make it a real feast.

SERVES 2

5 bulbs JERUSALEM ARTICHOKE, peeled
   and diced
2 tbsp ROQUEFORT CHEESE
Splash of CREAM
300g BLACK PUDDING
VEGETABLES, EDIBLE FLOWERS, SHOOTS,
   SEA HERBS and other seasonal additions

Peel the artichokes, dice, then simmer in water until cooked. They'll start to fall apart, which should take 20–25 minutes. Remove from the heat and pass through a tamis. Add the Roquefort and cream. Cook that out and reduce until it's a very thick veloute.

Now cook your black pudding. Pop it into a frying pan for four or five minutes until crisp. Remove it from the heat, drain, then pulse it through a food processor, to give you a soil texture. Set aside and keep it warm.

Now prepare your vegetables. Chargrill asparagus spears for two minutes on a very hot griddle, poach Chantenay carrots in dashi, add samphire, edible flowers, baby parsnips and whatever else is available. When they're cooked, remove and cut the bases at 90 degrees, so that they'll stand.

Assembly. Pour the veloute into the bowl, ensuring it's sufficiently thick for the vegetables and other elements to stand up in it. Scatter the black pudding soil across the top, so that it covers the veloute. Now stand your vegetables and herbs in the mixture, so that it looks like a garden.

You can add beetroot leaves, samphire, edible flowers, wheat grass and lots of other components that don't need to be cooked but which add freshness and decoration to the dish.

Carrot and Ginger Soup

Have you ever seen a bowl of soup as fresh and vibrant as this? Have you ever seen one as colourful and full of flavour? This is an intensely satisfying and brilliantly light bowl of soup. It combines delicious flavours with fresh, crunchy herbs and a luxurious duck egg. It's a meal in a bowl.

SERVES 6

10 CARROTS
2 sheets KOMBU
500g DRIED CEPS
2 ltrs WATER
5 large TOMATOES
6 EGGS

OPTIONAL EXTRAS
SEA ASTER
SEA BUCKTHORN
ICE LETTUCE

First sous-vide your duck egg by placing in a water bath at 62C for an hour, then refresh in ice-cold water. To make the dashi, add the kombu, ceps, water and tomatoes into a pan and simmer for 30 minutes, making sure you do not boil. In a separate pan, boil the carrots until tender. When cooked, purée in a food processor and add the carrot purée to the dashi. Pass through a fine tamis.

Assembly. Warm the dashi, but not above 60C, otherwise it will split. Place the sous-vide egg into a bowl then pour the dashi over, which will warm the egg. Randomly place a selection of the sea herbs around the egg.

1   2   3   4

5   6   7   8

Savoury garnishes

Attractive garnishes are an essential part of modern cuisine. Chefs in Japan and Thailand, for instance, spend long hours making their food look as beautiful as they can. They carve fruit and vegetables, refining dishes so that they are like works of art. Fish is trimmed so that it is millimetre-perfect. They recognised that eating is a sensate pleasure – and the visual stimulus is almost as important as taste. So we spend long hours making sure our dishes look as attractive as they can be – and that often involves garnishing them with delicious little herbs and flowers that add flavour and visual flair. Here's a handy guide to eight of our favourite garnishes.

1 Golden pea shoots. These pea shoots are grown in complete darkness to suppress the production of chlorophyll. They have a crisp texture and a sweet and nutty taste.

2 Micro-coriander. Micro-coriander is typically harvested after between 10 and 25 days of growth, and is intensely flavoured. It has an intense aromatic coriander flavour with slight anise and pepper notes.

3 Red amaranth. The striking colour of red amaranth is allied to a mild beetroot flavour, which makes it an ideal addition to stir-fries and egg dishes, or as an attractive garnish to meat.

4 Sea buckthorn. Sea buckthorn has been used in food and medicine for centuries in Russia and China. Its berries are quite tart, almost like sour orange with hints of mango. There are also notes of pineapple.

5 Sea beet. Sea beet is also known as wild spinach. It is a distant cousin of such foods as chard and sugar beet. The thick leaves give a more satisfying bite than spinach.

6 Viola flowers. These delicate flowers have bold colours and a very mild sweet-to-tart flavour. They are also known as pansy flowers.

7 Pea shoots. These tendrils have become ubiquitous in kitchens throughout the UK. They are an attractive addition to any meal and have a wonderful pea flavour, as well as a delicious crispness and crunch.

8 Micro-celery. These green feathery leaves work beautifully with meat and fish and can also be added to soups and salads. They have a stronger celery flavour than that of mature celery.

桃の木

FISH

Rules of fish

I love cooking with fish. It is *so* versatile. Raw, salted, seasoned, fried, poached, roasted, cured in citrus – there's almost no end of ways that you can cook it.

I love the delicate sweet-saltiness of scallop or lobster, the robust meaty texture of monkfish or the subtleties of sea bass or monk fish.

Most towns have a decent fishmonger, so that you don't have to rely on the supermarket. I'm fortunate in having an exceptional relationship with my local supplier – he drops in or calls me when he's expecting a delivery of the best-quality produce.

Rule number one, therefore, is to form a relationship with your fishmonger. Even if you only visit once a fortnight or once a month, get on speaking terms so that you get to find out what's in season and what's at its best.

If you're unable to do that, then follow these simple tips.

If you're buying whole fish, make sure the fish has clear, bright eyes. The eyes fade to grey the older a fish is. Dull-eyed fish may still be safe to eat, but it will be past its best.

Check out a fish's scales. Make sure they are still shiny. Some fish will be almost metallic, they should certainly be clean. If that colouration has gone and the fish is duller, then don't buy the fish.

There are other tell-tale signs. A fish should smell of the sea. If it smells unpleasant, it *is* unpleasant, so don't buy it. That's the bottom line. The moment a fish smells fishy is the moment to put it back on the counter.

Finally, look at the gills. You want a rich red – almost crimson – colour. The gills of old fish will fade.

If you're buying fillets of fish, your checks are reduced. Press the meat with your thumb; it should be resilient so that your thumbprint soon disappears. If the thumbprint remains, move on. Again, check for a fresh, non-pungent smell and make sure the flesh looks vibrant. Finally, check the surface for liquid. If it's fresh, any liquid will be clear. If it's milky, it's starting to rot.

If you're buying shellfish, make sure it's fresh. Fishmongers with a high turnover are best – they ship in and ship out while it's still fresh. If you're buying live scallops or clams, try tapping the shell. You'll notice it close a little more tightly, as a defence mechanism. If your clams or mussels do not open after cooking, thrown them away. If you're buying scallops, buy hand-dived, rather than dredged – the dredging process destroys the sea bed.

If you're buying prawns or crayfish, either buy very fresh or buy frozen. Squid and octopus also freeze well.

The bottom line is this: if it smells of the sea and looks fresh, you're onto a winner. If not, avoid it.

The Earth and the Sea

The sublime kombu-infused dashi, steeped in tomato liquor, gives this dish a mesmerising colour and flavour. Fresh samphire, scallop and herbs make it scintillatingly fresh. The preparation for this can take up to a day.

FOR TWO TO SHARE

500ml DASHI, infused with kombu
Handful SHIITAKE MUSHROOMS
800g PLUM OR BEEF TOMATOES
RICE-WINE VINEGAR
SOY SAUCE
MIRIN
KATSUOBUSHI
2 SCALLOPS
ASSORTED CAVIAR
SAMPHIRE
SEASONAL SEA HERBS

OPTIONAL EXTRAS
NASTURTIUM FLOWERS
CHILLI SHRIMP OIL
RED-VEIN SORREL

Take 500ml of dashi and simmer. Add kombu and infuse. Add a few shiitake mushrooms and 200g of the tomatoes. Simmer lightly, then remove from heat and strain. Cover the remaining shiitake mushrooms with rice wine vinegar, seasoned with a little soy sauce and a few splashes of mirin. Leave to pickle and set aside.

Add a tbsp of katsuobushi to your warm dashi and leave for between three to five minutes, depending on how smokey you like it. Drain. Now simmer the dashi very, very slowly, eventually reducing by about half. Leave to stand.

In a food processor, blend the remaining tomatoes. Strain through muslin for at least 12 hours. Add the resulting pure tomato essence to your dashi and simmer to reduce by half. You will be left with a very light, vibrant and clear golden, orange dashi. Pour your dashi into a lidded donabe* pot and keep warm. Add rapeseed oil to a hot pan, take your scallops and slice through so they are half the thickness. Cook for 60–70 seconds on each side. Season, then place on a cloth for a minute to rest.

Sprinkle sea herbs, such as sea beet, ice lettuce and sea buckthorn into your dashi, as well as samphire. Put the scallops into the pot, then add a tsp of the caviar of your choice. Garnish with nasturtium flowers and season with droplets of chilli shrimp oil.

*NB: A donabe pot is an earthenware vessel, glazed inside, that can be used over an open flame.

72

The Sleeping Buddha

Fresh, crisp and marrying contrasting textures with ring-a-ding-ding flavours, this is a crowd-pleasing plate. Turn the heat up or down, according to preference, by adding more or less togarashi and wasabi.

FOR 1 SERVING
4 deveined PRAWN TAILS
1 large stalk CAVOLO NERO
4 tbsp POLENTA
1 tbsp TOGARASHI
1 tbsp WASABI POWDER
TEMPURA BATTER (p49)
Slice of LIME

FOR THE DRESSING
100ml THAI SWEET CHILLI
1 tbsp WHITE MISO
½ tsp SOY SAUCE
5g XANTHAN GUM
5g HY FOAMER

Leave the stalk in your cavolo nero, which will give it better rigidity and help it to sit more easily on the plate.

Mix your polenta with the wasabi and togarashi powders. If you want more heat, add more togarashi powder. If you want more horseradish bite, add extra wasabi.

Make your dressing. Blend sweet chilli with white miso, soy sauce and the xanthan gum and hy foamer, which can both be purchased from outlets such as MSK. Add a little water if it's too thick. It will change to a slightly foamy consistency, almost like a light-coloured salad cream texture. Pop into the fridge.

Dip the cavolo nero into the tempura batter and fry at 170C until crisp, for three minutes or so. It should be nice and crisp.

Dip the shrimps into the tempura then roll in the polenta-wasabi-togarashi mix. Fry for three or four minutes, remove from the fryer and drain.

Assembly. I like to serve this on a slate. Stand the tempura-ed cavolo on its side, create a stack of prawns by holding together with a skewer, garnishing with lime. Drizzle the dressing across the plate.

MOMO NO KI

Shrimp and Grits

Appearances can be deceptive. While this dish looks pretty simple – starch, leaf, prawns and dressing – a lot of work goes into it. Don't be put off by that, the rewards are huge.

SERVES 4

300g POPCORN KERNELS
800ml MILK
250g UNSALTED BUTTER
2–3 tbsps RAPESEED OIL
12 DEVEINED PRAWNS
1 small BIRD'S-EYE CHILLI
500ml DASHI
Grated PECORINO
4 SEABEET LEAVES – use whatever is
   available

We'll start with the grits because they're the hardest. Take the popcorn kernels and put a pan on the heat to get nice and warm. Put in a couple of tbsps of oil and add your popcorn kernels. Make sure there's a lid on it: then it will be pop, pop, pop, pop, pop. Once it's all popped, put it to one side.

In a separate pan, simmer the milk with the butter. Once the butter's melted, take small batches of the popcorn and dunk it into the milk-and-butter mix. Blanch it for up to a minute, until the popcorn is soggy. Once the whole batch is done, pop the soggy popcorn into a tamis and pass it through. This will take a while. Just have patience and push it through, it's worth the effort. These are our 'grits'. Season to taste. The objective is to add as much butter and seasoning as it can take. Just stir it through and it will absorb all that loveliness. If you take a spoon and taste it, it should have the texture of polenta but the taste of popcorn. Pop that to one side.

Now take your cleaned, deveined prawns and pop into a pan of dashi. Simmer for four minutes, until cooked through. Finely chop your bird's-eye chilli, then drop into the dashi and simmer. Grate three tbsps of pecorino into the grits, which will help it to coalesce and also give it extra flavour.

Assembly. Spoon a quenelle of grits into the bottom of the bowl. Place a seabeet leaf on top. Place three prawns above. Drizzle with a little of the dashi and bird's-eye chilli dressing and grate over more pecorino. That's the dish.

Da Umami Bomb

Looks can be deceptive. While Da Umami Bomb looks as pretty as a picture, it's an explosive plate. Few dishes pack as powerful a punch.

SERVES 1
175g piece of SALMON FILLET, scaled
50g BLONDE MISO
65g BUTTER
¼ SWEET POTATO
200ml DASHI
VARIEGATED KALES
ASPARAGUS SPEARS
SPRING ONIONS
BULGOGI SAUCE

Soften the butter and mix it with about 50g of miso to form a buttery paste. Apply that to your salmon and pop it in the fridge.

Cut a sweet potato into 2cm dice. Take half a dozen and simmer in a pan of dashi, until al dente. Pop to one side.

Blanch kale leaves and set aside. Douse asparagus spears and spring onions with rapeseed oil, then chargrill until al dente.

Assembly. Take the pieces of sweet potato fondant and place on the bottom of the plate. Place the blanched kales on top. Squeeze a little bulgogi sauce on top. Now roast off the salmon in your pan, which should take between seven and nine minutes, depending on the size and thickness. The miso butter will help to give it a lovely golden brown crust.

Cut the asparagus into four and arrange as shown. Drape the spring onions on top and give it another quick squirt of bulgogi.

This dish works beautifully with a crisp apple kimchi salad (p32).

78

Dinga Magoo

We use the same cooking technique here as we do for The Wylie (p97), by making a huge, long, lobster noodle. You must work quickly when doing so, because you don't want there too be so much friction on the blades of your processor that they generate heat and start to cook the raw lobster.

SERVES 1

225g RAW LOBSTER MEAT
1½ tsp ACTIVA EB
½ tsp CHILLI SHRIMP OIL
1 tsp CHICKEN POWDER
Knob of BUTTER
2 SPRING ONIONS, finely chopped
1 CLOVE OF GARLIC, finely diced
SOY SAUCE
PICKLED PINK GINGER
SESAME SEEDS

Take the raw meat from the lobster. Split an uncooked lobster down the middle of the head, or let your fishmonger do it for you. Remove the tail meat, leaving the claw intact: it must be raw, not be pre-cooked. Also add the tamale and roe, which give it extra flavour.

Now it's time to turn your lobster meat into noodles. So quickly whizz them through a food processor with the Activa EB, chilli shrimp oil and chicken powder. Once minced, pass through a tamis, then pipe into a long line, 3mm thick.

Now take the residual shell, which still has the claw attached. Boil that for eight minutes, then remove and pop to one side.

Add a little butter to a wok and then sauté your spring onion and garlic, adding a little soy to season. Cut your noodle into lengths, then throw it into the wok to cook through.

Assembly. Place the noodles back into the shell, crack open the claw, to give you a delicious nugget of meat, then garnish with pickled pink ginger, sesame seeds and more spring onion, as desired. It's a very simple dish, once you've made the noodle.

The Fish, the Pig and the Egg

This is another reinterpretation of a classic surf and turf. It's a million times lighter, more flavoursome and more nourishing than traditional versions.

SERVES 1

150–200g MONKFISH LOIN
1 slice IBERICO HAM
1 tsp ACTIVA EB
1 tsp TOBBIKO ORANGE CAVIAR
1 tsp TOBBIKO YELLOW CAVIAR
RAPESEED OIL
125g RISOTTO RICE (or NISHIKI RICE)
1 large SHALLOT, finely diced
1 clove GARLIC, finely diced
Knob of BUTTER
250ml DASHI
Single-serving sachet of SQUID INK
Small handful of PARMESAN
Trimmings of CRAYFISH, LOBSTER or
  PRAWN
VARIEGATED KALE LEAVES
ASPARAGUS SPEARS

Activa EB is more commonly known as meatglue. It is used to bond raw and cooked meats. Take a tsp of Activa EB and sprinkle it over the monkfish loin. Now take a long, thin piece of Iberico ham and wrap it around the loin. Wrap tightly in cling film, to create a torchon, and pop it in the fridge for an hour. Poach your torchon, while it's still wrapped in film, in simmering water for around 20 minutes. Remove from the cling film and let it rest.

Wash your rice three times. In a separate pan, soften the shallot and garlic in butter. Add dashi, a little at a time, until the rice becomes al dente. Now add the squid ink (get it from your fishmonger), which will turn the rice black. Adjust the seasoning, adding dashi and butter until satisfied.

Add in your diced lobster, prawn or crayfish trimmings and finish with a little parmesan to make it cohesive and bring it together.

Now brown off your ham/monkfish, in a hot pan with a knob of butter. Slice into roundels approximately 3cm thick.

Blanch the variegated kale for 90 seconds and chargrill the asparagus for two minutes.

Assembly. Put risotto on the bottom of plate and sprinkle parmesan over it. Add the kales. Then put the roundels of monkfish and ham on top. Place asparagus around and garnish with caviars and a little squeeze of rapeseed oil.

MOMO·NO·KI

The Miyabi

I love the delicate simplicity of Asian food and The Miyabi encapsulates many of those qualities. Brimful of flavour, visually stunning and punching above its weight, this is perfect as an appetiser or starter, or can be scaled-up to a main. (I created this dish for my wife Jo; it is named after the restaurant in Bangkok where we got engaged.)

SERVES 4 AS A STARTER

3 tbsp MAYONNAISE (homemade is best)
Generous pinch of WASABI POWDER
1 tsp BLACK SESAME SEEDS
4 tbsp KIMCHI (p32)
3 SPRING ONIONS, finely sliced
6 SCALLOPS
4 tbsp POLENTA
1 tbsp TOGARASHI
TEMPURA BATTER (p49)
EDIBLE FLOWERS or MICROSHOOTS

First, make your dressing. Combine the mayonnaise with toasted black sesame seeds and wasabi powder. Adjust to suit your palate. Add a little of the wasabi powder at a time. Pop to one side.

Now make a kimchi slaw, by taking shredded kimchi and finely sliced spring onions. Set aside.

Slice your scallops through the middle, so that they're half as fat. Pat dry, immerse in tempura, then dredge through well-mixed polenta and togarashi, until fully coated. Deep fry at 170C for two or three minutes. Season with sea salt.

Assembly. Stick your spoons to the plate, as shown, using the mayonnaise. Pop the togarashi scallops onto the spoons, heap a little mayonnaise on top and garnish with edible flowers or micro-coriander.

MOMO·NO·KI

Seascape, AKA Tonka Toys

The colours on this dish are remarkable. Reds, greens and purples battle it out with the intense, deep hues of the rare-cooked tuna; not forgetting the dramatic scorch marks which feature across the top. A visual feast; Seascape – lovingly nicknamed Tonka Toys – also packs a flavoursome punch. It tastes as good as it looks.

SERVES 1

200g TUNA STEAK
8g HY FOAMER
8g XANTHAN GUM
½ tsp WASABI POWDER
3 TONKA BEANS
2 tbsp SWEET CHILLI
2 tbsp BULGOGI
2 × 5mm slices SWEET POTATO
BEETROOT POWDER
SESAME OIL
Handful of EDAMAME BEANS
6 FRENCH BEANS
6 VARIEGATED KALE LEAVES
Knob of BUTTER
¼ tsp MISO
FISH SAUCE
SEA HERBS to garnish

Take your tuna and rub it with sesame oil. Pop it in the fridge to infuse, while you prepare your other elements. Start with your tonka bean and wasabi dressing, by mixing your hy foamer, xanthan gum, wasabi powder, tonka beans (which you should first grate on a microplane), sweet chilli and bulgogi. Add water, a little at a time, mixing continuously until it starts to foam, then blitz in a food processor or grinder. That leaves us with a nice foam to dress the tuna with.

Now make your sweet potato sable. Cut the slices of sweet potato into triangles, as pictured. Poach them in dashi and then sprinkle with beetroot powder, which gives them a vivid red-purple colour.

Prepare your garnish. Squirt a little sesame oil into a bowl, throw in a generous handful of edamame beans, cut the French beans into small pieces and add, then toss in some variegated kale leaves. Toss in a pan with a knob of butter and the miso, then set aside.

Assembly. Heat the chargrill so that it's smoking hot, then sear the tuna for 1½–2 minutes on either side. Take off the heat and allow to rest. Drizzle with tonka bean and wasabi dressing. Now take the miso-buttered vegetables to the plate. Decorate with the triangles of sweet potato sable and garnish with sea herbs such as sea beet, ice lettuce and sea buckthorn, and a splash of fish sauce.

This can be served with variegated kale, fried at 150C until crisp.

Bass and Beats

Okay, okay. Forgive the spelling. We couldn't resist the play on words. Bass and Beats – or, if you prefer, beets, is a flavoursome dish that brings out the best in a glorious piece of fresh sea bass. The addition of sweet, earthy beetroot risotto and plenty of sea herbs elevates the dish.

SERVES 1

175g FILLET OF SEA BASS, SCALED, BONED AND TRIMMED

GHEE

100g NISHIKI RICE

250ML DASHI

1 SHALLOT, finely diced

Splash of RAPESEED OIL

1 tbsp BEETROOT POWDER

2 slices of either SERRANO, PARMA or IBERICO HAM

30g WHOLE BLANCHED ALMONDS

50g CAPERS

RICE WINE VINEGAR

Dash of MIRIN

Knob of BUTTER

1 tbsp grated PARMESAN

SEA HERBS, eg SEA BUCKTHORN, ICE LETTUCE and SEA BEETS

RAPESEED OIL

Bring a frying pan of ghee up to a heat of 50–60C. Then add the sea bass, skin-side up, and gently poach it for seven or eight minutes. (You could cook the fish under the grill, making sure the heat is not too ferocious.) Once it's cooked, let it rest in the ghee.

Wash the rice well. Heat up the shallot with a splash of rapeseed oil. Add the rice, and let it out with dashi. Add the beetroot powder (available from MSK). Finish the risotto with butter and parmesan and adjust the seasoning.

Make the ham crisps. Cook the ham slowly in a low oven or, if you're pushed for time, simply fry off the slices of ham in a 180C fryer for a couple of minutes. Dry on kitchen paper.

Rub the almonds with rapeseed oil, then gently grill. For the twice-roast flavour, pop them into the oven for three minutes at 180C. When they've cooled down slightly, just run your knife through them and break them up a little.

Rinse the capers, then steep them in rice wine vinegar and mirin, to taste.

Assembly. Plate the risotto and place your ham crisps on top. The sea bass will be very delicate, so place it on top, being careful not to break it. Discard the vinegar and mirin from your capers, spooning the capers over. Sprinkle on the almonds and garnish with sea herbs. Add a splash of rapeseed oil and microherbs to finish.

88
MOMO·NO·KI

It's Pasta Jim, but not as We Know it

Smokey tofu, deeply satisfying seared tuna, a firecracker marinade and light ribbons of cucumber 'pasta' make this an absolute classic. It's presented beautifully and deliciously light.

SERVES 2

200g TUNA LOIN
SESAME OIL
15cm CUCUMBER
200g SMOKED TOFU
SOY SAUCE
Variety of CAVIARS
EDIBLE FLOWERS
RAPESEED OIL
PONZU
½ tsp MIRIN
½ tsp BULGOGI

Make sure your tuna loin is red and fresh. Rub it with sesame oil and pop to one side. Get a chargrill pan seriously hot. Now cook the tuna for 90 seconds each side, then pop it in the fridge to cool down.

Take a mandolin and slice eight long strips of peeled cucumber. Pop those to one side. Make a small dice with the rest of the cucumber. Crumble the tofu and combine, then season with a splash of soy sauce. Pop it in the fridge.

Make a dressing for your tuna tataki. Take ½ tsp of rapeseed and two squirts of sesame oil. Add a little ponzu (a citrus-based sauce available in Asian supermarkets). Add the mirin and bulgogi and combine, then brush it onto the tuna.

Assembly. To make the cannelloni, take six ribbons of cucumber and roll them around the smoked tofu and diced cucumber. The remaining two ribbons are cut neatly into oblongs and laid flat on the plate. The cannelloni will stand on those. It's tricky to roll the cannelloni, so you may need to put a skewer through them to hold them together. Garnish each with a different caviar, so use Tabiko green, salmon or pike roe. Garnish further with edible flowers.

Take your tuna out of the fridge and cut neat 3mm slices. Trim off the ends so that they look perfect. Six pieces will give you two dishes.

Surf and Turf, AKA The Sea Scratching

Few dishes are quite as pretty as the sea scratching. It's a real crowd pleaser – and it tastes even better than it looks. We use three specialist products (available from MSK) so you'll need to spend a while sourcing ingredients if you want to replicate this, or use equivalent alternatives. We make a sweetcorn dashi to offset the flavours of the scallop, which is hidden from view by puffed-up pork scratchings. There's texture, colour and complementary flavours in this masterpiece of a dish.

SERVES 1

1 large SCALLOP, roe discarded
FLAT PORK CRACKLING RINDS
MALT VINEGAR POWDER
BUTTER POWDER
1 sheet KOMBU
100g BUTTER
1 quantity TEMPURA MIX (p49)

Season your scallop with ground white pepper and a little rapeseed oil. Pop it to one side.

Make your sweetcorn dashi by taking a whole sweetcorn and simmering in water with a sheet of kombu. Once cooked, remove the corn and strip off the kernels. Put them into a food processor with the butter, then pass it through a fine tamis. Leave to cool.

Take the scallop, lightly tempura it and pop it in the fryer for one minute. Remove from the fryer and adhere between six and eight pork rinds to the outside. Now pop that back into the fryer for two or three minutes, putting another basket on top to make sure the pork rinds stick to the tempura. When it's nicely puffed up, remove it from the fryer and rest.

Assembly. Reheat the corn and pop that into a bowl. Place the scallop on top and then sieve a little of the vinegar powder and butter powder over. They are quite strong, so go easy. They're being used as half-garnish, half-flavour. Garnish with pansies and other edible flowers. In this instance, I've served the dish with corn purée dashi and spinach chlorophyll (p117).

92

MOMO·NO·KI

Clams and Ham

There are myriad versions of surf and turf and this one's a real belter. Razor clams are an underused ingredient, though I think they're delicious. They have a scallop-like texture and a sweet-salty flavour. The addition of salty ham provides a perfect counterpoint.

SERVES 1

2 RAZOR CLAMS
8 NORMAL CLAMS
1 clove GARLIC, finely chopped
2 SHALLOTS, finely chopped
1 TOMATO, skinned, cored and diced
Knob of BUTTER
50g CHORIZO, cut into 5mm dice
150g pre-cooked BLACK-EYED BEANS
1 tsp XO SAUCE
¼ small BIRD'S-EYE CHILLI, finely diced
3 leaves CAVOLO NERO

OPTIONAL EXTRAS
MICROHERBS

Take the razor clams and give them a liberal squirt of rapeseed oil, then pop them under the grill. The clams will start to open. When they do, take them out. They should take 1½–2 minutes under a 160C grill. Remove the gut sac and discard. Trim the clam, cut into three and pop to one side.

In a frying pan add rapeseed oil, garlic and shallots. Add your tomato dice. Now add a little butter and throw in your chorizo dice. Once they start to go brown, add the black-eyed beans. Don't be afraid to give it plenty of vigorous heat.

Throw in your regular clams, turn down the heat and put a saucepan lid on top, to keep in the steam. This will help to cook the clams and their shells will start to open. Discard any that don't open.

When the clams are open, the dish is ready to be seasoned. Add the XO sauce and bird's-eye chilli. Thrown in cavolo nero and toss it through. Put your razor clam meat back in, to finish off.

Assembly. Take the razor clam shells and clean. Now gently spoon the mix into the shells. Add the other clams to the plate, spoon the black-eyed beans around the plate. Garnish with microherbs.

94

The Momo·No·Ki Bacalao–Macalao . . .

. . . it depends on how you serve it! The preparation of the cod is central to this dish. It creates a cut of fish that is firm to touch and intensely flavoured, while being beautifully complemented by a rich, buttery tomato sauce. Bacalao is a Portugese dish with chorizo, while Macalao is a Chinese version.

SERVES 1

150g COD
SEA SALT
100G CHORIZO
100G CHINESE SAUSAGE
BUTTER-NESCA SAUCE (p97)
SAGE LEAVES
BASIL LEAVES

Take a piece of cod and cut it so that it's rectangular. I like a size around 4cm × 2cm × 2cm, with the skin left on. Cover in sea salt and put on a draining board or wooden board. This helps to remove the moisture. After five minutes, wash the salt off and pat dry. You will notice that the fish has firmed up. Pop it into the fridge for an hour and leave; it will firm up even more.

Now make a butter-nesca sauce, which uses the same method as the one we make for The Wylie (p97). Once your butter-nesca sauce is made, you can add small dice of either Chinese sausage or Iberico chorizo. That's the turning point for the dish. Bacalao is served with crispy sage leaves, which are fried off for 30 seconds. Macalao is served with crispy basil leaves, which also take 30 seconds in the fryer.

Now cook the fish. Rub it with rapeseed oil then pop it onto a tray on the bottom part of the grill and gently toast for eight minutes, so that it falls apart. Cooking times will vary, depending on your grill, so you might take much longer, almost double that time. You can add more butter, to prevent it drying out.

Assembly. Deep-fry the sage and basil leaves. Place the sauce on the bottom of the bowl, add the fish and garnish with the deep-fried leaves.

The Wylie

This is one of the most complicated dishes that I cook and should only be attempted by advanced home cooks, or professionals. It was inspired by the great chef Wylie Dufresne, at WD-50, in Manhattan. I've created a rich, buttery 'butter-nesca' sauce to go with it, which is a spin on the conventional puttanesca variety.

SERVES 2

225g DEVEINED PRAWNS
1½ tsp ACTIVA EB
½ tbsp CHILLI SHRIMP OIL
CHICKEN POWDER
2 × 200g SWORDFISH FILLETS
2 BEEF TOMATOES
2 SHALLOTS, finely diced
RICE-WINE VINEGAR
RAPESEED OIL
Pinch of SUGAR
100g BUTTER
Handful of SAMPHIRE
PINK KALE LEAVES
Finely cut SPRING ONION

Wylie Dufresne used to work for Heston Blumenthal and was among the first chefs to start working with meat glue, or protein glue, which is called transglutaminase (Activa EB). The product can be bought from companies such as MSK, or in small quantities from Amazon.

First, we make our prawn noodles. Take 225g of spotlessly clean prawns and blitz in a food processor with the Activa EB, chilli shrimp oil and a tsp of chicken powder.

Work quickly, otherwise the blades will heat and cook the prawns. Pass through a tamis, so that it's very fine and smooth, then pipe into long lines, 3mm thick. I cook at 56C in a sous-vide machine, but you can poach in simmering water. Remove and refresh in ice water. Set aside.

Season your swordfish with sesame oil and set aside.

Now it's time to make the butter-nesca sauce. Take your beef tomatoes, slit the skin at the base, blanch in boiling water, refresh then peel. Remove the core, then dice them.

Sweat the shallots in rapeseed oil and add a tbsp of chicken powder, a splash of rice-wine vinegar and a generous pinch of sugar, which gets the whole umami thing going on. Add in the garlic and tomato. You need to work out the dynamics to get the right flavour, so keep tasting. Different tomatoes will have different flavours, depending on the season and other variables. So continue to taste and test.

Continued ➲

⊃ Now we're going to add butter, but we don't want it to fully split. Turn down the heat and start whisking in cold butter; all of a sudden the sauce will start to come together. Keep tasting to get a salty-sweet balance.

Once our sauce is complete, put it in a cup. Now take a smoke gun*, clingfilm the top of the cup and burn maple or hickory wood chips, infusing the sauce with smoke. Do that two or three times, stirring between each. You must keep the clingfilm in place throughout, to help the smoke infuse.

Now sear the swordfish steaks in a hot pan for about two-and-a-half minutes each side, depending on the thickness. Rest.

Reheat the smokey butter-nesca sauce. Cut the prawn noodles into appropriate lengths. Take samphire, finely shredded spring onion and a couple of pieces of blanched pink kale and drizzle with rapeseed oil.

Assembly. Take the shrimp noodles and cover with butter-nesca sauce. Place the swordfish on top and dress with kale, spring onion and samphire, garnishing with microherbs.

* Don't worry about using the smoking gun. They're simple to use and add plenty of flavour to your dish. In essence, you set light to wood chips, then feed a tube into the dish that you're making. Smoky air is pumped into the dish. If you're unsure, refer to the manufacturer's instructions.

桃の木

MOMO·NO·KI

MEAT

Rules of meat

The rules of meat are fairly similar to the rules of fish. The best thing you can do is to strike up a good relationship with your butcher. Here in Shropshire, and the counties that surround us, we're blessed with a real abundance. Take time to get to know them.

You get what you pay for, so if you're being offered a deal that seems too good to be true, it probably is. There are exceptions to this, of course, depending on the season. Your butcher might receive a high volume of a particular animal, or have a large amount of a particular cut, such as shin, which other people don't want, so keep your eyes peeled. Just be sure about what you're buying before you part with your cash.

If you're buying from supermarkets or other outlets, make sure you check the label. Just because it says UK, doesn't mean it was reared here. The UK imports huge volumes of meat from Argentina, New Zealand, Australia and other parts of the world, so be sure you check its country of origin – not the country where it's been processed.

Look for marbling in your meat. Marbling is indicative of fat content, which helps to keep the meat moist and also gives it plenty of flavour. There are a few breeds which marble particularly well: if you're buying beef, for instance – and budget is no hindrance – then go for Longhorn or even Wagyu, which is extremely popular in Japan and Australia.

Not all cuts are equal. Fillets are lean and have less fat content, so take less cooking. Cheaper cuts – shin, oxtail, trotters or heads, say – take a lot more work – but the rewards make them worth it. Meat with a low percentage of fat and connective tissue cooks more quickly than meat with a higher percentage, which may need slow cooking and braising.

Learn how to confit meat such as pork shoulder or belly pork. Confit involves poaching the meat in fat – it could be duck fat, rapeseed oil or other animal or vegetable fats – for longer periods of time. You can add salt, pepper, thyme and other aromatics to the mix – star anise works well with a number of confit dishes I make. Cooking times vary, but it's not uncommon to confit duck legs or pork shoulder for between two and three hours. You're waiting for the meat to fall away and be deliciously, meltingly soft when you remove it.

Learning good techniques for cooking belly pork is important. Some like to slow cook, regularly basting, so that the fat gently works its own way through the meat. You can poach the meat with carrots, celery, onions and aromatics such as thyme, sage, and bay, or Asian spices including five-spice or star anise. Cooking times will vary, depending on the size of the cut and the method you use.

104

MOMO·NO·KI

The Uncle Ho – Tête Offensive

This is one of the more complicated dishes. You'll be able to pick up a pig's head from your butcher – if you're lucky, they might not even charge you – and the results are spectacular. I use chicken powder, which is popular in Asian cultures. We literally can't make enough stocks to keep up, so we use that.

SERVES 4

1 PIG'S HEAD
3 tbsp CHICKEN POWDER
1 tbsp FIVE-SPICE POWDER
1 tbsp SOY SAUCE
SESAME OIL
CHILLI SHRIMP OIL
250g UNSALTED BUTTER
125g SHALLOTS, finely chopped
2 cloves GARLIC, finely chopped
1 BIRD'S-EYE CHILLI, finely chopped
25g GRATED GINGER
200g CARROTS
200ml RICE-WINE VINEGAR
3 tbsp SOY SAUCE
½ tsp CHILLI SEEDS
1 tsp BLACK SESAME SEEDS
½ tsp SHA CHA SAUCE
1 slice SOURDOUGH BREAD
BABY BASIL LEAVES

Immerse the pig's head – cleaned, shaved and excess hair burned off with a blowtorch – in a heavily salted pan of water. Add the chicken powder, five-spice, soy sauce, sesame oil and chili shrimp oil. Simmer for three hours. The pig's head will start to fall apart. Allow it to cool. Pick all the skin off and put that to one side. Remove the cheeks and the meat behind the head, then discard the bones. Be thorough as you clean the meat, removing all bone and cartilage.

Pop the meat into a food processor with a pack of softened butter and pulse with the chopped shallots and garlic. Add the chilli and grated ginger and pulse until the mixture has a pâté-like texture. Check the seasoning, ensuring the five-spice comes through. If it does not, add a little more. Transfer the mixture to a terrine mould and pop into the fridge.

Grate your carrots. Add the rice-wine vinegar, mirin and soy, then the chilli seeds and black sesame seeds. Put it in on the stove for three or four minutes to infuse. Now simmer and add the sha cha sauce. Season with sesame oil. Cool.

Assembly. Slice a piece of terrine and place on top of the sourdough toast. The toast and tête de cochon should both be around 2cm thick. Now swish the pickle across the plate.

You can add deep-fried baby basil leaves to finish, maybe with extra sha cha sauce.

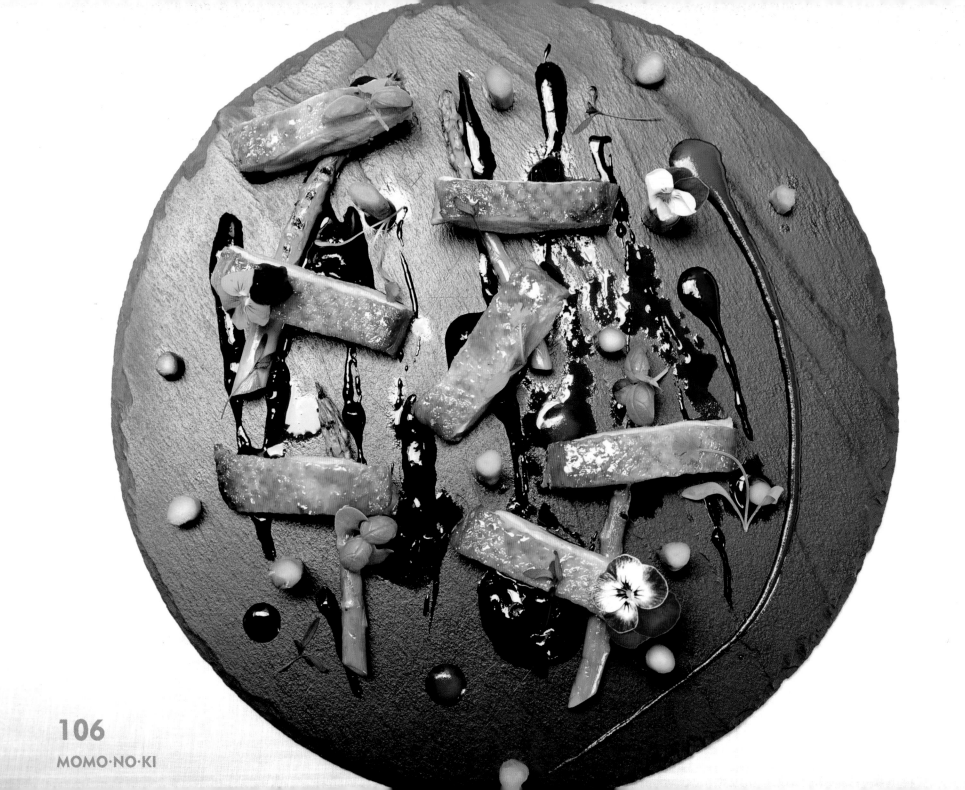

The Duck Hunter

This is a visually stunning dish that combines myriad complementary flavours and a delightful presentation. It's a surprisingly light duck dish, with the absence of carbohydrates.

200–250g breast of GRESSINGHAM DUCK
1 tbsp HONEY or MAPLE SYRUP
1 tsp SOUR CHERRY COMPOUND
2 tbsp CHICKEN STOCK
Knob of BUTTER
ASPARAGUS
RAPESEED OIL

OPTIONAL EXTRAS
This dish goes beautifully with colcannon
   dauphinoise potato, which is dauphinoise
   with the addition of spring onions (try
   telling that to an Irishman . . .)
EDIBLE FLOWERS and MICROHERBS
GREEN APPLE PUREE, for garnish

Season the duck breast with salt and pepper. I cook mine with thyme in a vacpac bag, in a sous-vide machine, for an hour at 56C. You can cook by scoring the breast, seasoning and frying skin-side down in a pan until the fat turns golden brown. That can take up to seven minutes – don't burn it – then turn over and cook the other side for two minutes. Now pop it into a preheated 190C oven for six minutes for rare, nine for medium and 12 for well done. Rest for eight minutes. There are a lot of variables, including the meat, type of oven and fat content, so use all of this as a guide.

If you've used a sous-vide machine, you'll need to pan-fry your duck for two minutes each side, to finish. Glaze the skin with maple syrup or honey. They gave different flavour profiles, but both give a lovely glaze and shine.

I make a sour cherry reduction (using MSK's extremely sour cherry compound, which I add to the duck juices in the pan), adding in a little chicken stock to finish and butter if it needs it.

Coat your asparagus with rapeseed oil and chargrill for two or three minutes.

Assembly. Cut the duck into seven or eight pieces and arrange on the slate. Swish the sour cherry reduction and apple purée (if using) between. Cut the asparagus ends so that it stands up. Garnish with edible flowers, micro-coriander and micro-basil.

MOMO·NO·KI

The Sin Bin

There's a simply quality that south-east Asian food has in abundance and it's this: flavour. There are times when you have to work really hard to create a delicate balance of complementary flavours – and then there are times when it seems to come easy. The Sin Bin is a dish that seems almost effortless and yet the results are sublime.

SERVES 1

3cm square piece (or larger, if you can
   manage it) of CONFIT BELLY PORK
1 tsp SOUR CHERRY COMPOUND
1 tbsp HOISIN SAUCE
50g CUCUMBER
½ tsp PRESERVED KOMBU
1 tsp MIRIN
½ tsp WHITE-WINE VINEGAR
2 pieces KALE

OPTIONAL EXTRA
PICKLED PINK GINGER

Make sure the bottom of the belly pork is flat, so that it will stand on a plate, then pop it into a 150C fryer for three of four minutes, so that the skin crisps up. Remove, salt the skin and leave to drain and rest.

Mix the sour cherry compound (I get mine from MSK) with the hoisin. This is very much to taste. You're looking to achieve a plate with an equal balance of salt, sour and sweet, so you need to balance this using your own tastebuds. I find I want more hoisin than cherry, because I like the saltiness of hoisin. Set aside.

Now take a cucumber piece and dice it. Add some preserved kombu, which is edible kelp. Add the mirin and white-wine vinegar. Mix that together and let it sit for a few minutes.

Fry off the kale. It will spit, so be careful. It will take 60–90 seconds. Pop onto kitchen paper and let it dry.

Assembly. Swipe the cherry hoisin onto the plate. Pop the pork beside it. Add the cucumber relish and kale, as shown. Then tweezer-on pickled pink ginger, which breaks up the fattiness and the saltiness.

MOMO·NO·KI

Le Petit Cochon

SERVES 1

200g CONFIT BELLY PORK
PLAIN FLOUR
1 EGG, beaten
100g PANKO BREADCRUMBS
75g BRUSSELS SPROUTS
75g CURED COUNTRY HAM
75g EDAMAME BEANS
75g SWEETCORN KERNELS
1 SPRING ONION, cut into small pieces
A dash of FISH SAUCE
A little WHITE-WINE VINEGAR
A dash of MIRIN
1 tbsp BLACK SESAME SEEDS

This method is quite similar to that for Taishoken Ramen or The 3AM. We take a cut of pork and trim it into an oblong, so that it will stand on its end. Then dunk it in a mixture of egg and flour, then dredge that through Panko breadcrumbs, ensuring the meat is evenly coated. Pop that into the deep-fat fryer for four minutes, taking it out when it's crispy and golden brown. Allow to rest.

Now we take our Brussels sprouts (we want small ones so that we don't have to cross-cut them along the bottom). The objective is to keep them intact, so that they're nice and crunchy. We're not looking for those horrible, overcooked bullets that people eat on Christmas Day. Add a little rapeseed oil to a pan or wok and start to fry. Cut your ham into lardons and add them to the pan. Turn up the heat. The moisture from the sprouts will help the ham to cook. Now throw in sweetcorn kernels, edamame beans and the spring onion.

Add fish sauce, white wine vinegar and mirin, to give it a little sweetness.

Assembly. Cut the pork, as shown. Arrange the ham and greens around it and then dress with black sesame seeds.

Lonesome Pine

Food should take you on a journey – and few dishes do that as well as the Lonesome Pine. You can literally taste the wild, natural flavours in every mouthful. The essence of pine and smokey bay leaves just add to the mystique.

SERVES 2
300g REINDEER (or VENISON) LOIN
250g MULTI-GRAIN PORRIDGE, including
   pearl barley, quinoa and other grains
330g CHICKEN STOCK
2 tbsp SHOYU-DASHI
RAPESEED OIL
60g BUTTER
SIBERIAN PINE FLAVOUR DROPS
4 BAY LEAVES
2 tbsp MEDLAR (or QUINCE) JELLY or
   similar
125g BUTTER

Trim and clean your piece of meat. Marinade in salt and pepper then brush with rapeseed oil. Set aside.

Now make your multi-grain porridge. Simmer in chicken stock, until al dente, then roughly pulse in a food processor, to give a thick porridge consistency. Now add shuyo-dashi, which has bags of umami flavour. Add butter and season with salt and pepper. Trust your instincts as regards the volume of liquid: some grains will be more readily absorbant than others. Now add a few drop of Siberian pine flavour, but be really careful when you're seasoning. You only need a small amount, to give a hint of taste. Blanch the bay leaves and shred. Add to the porridge, then pulse once more in the food processor. Set aside.

Put your cast-iron skillet onto a high heat, season the meat and sear for four minutes on each side. Take it out, add butter and let it rest.

Now finish your porridge. You want to add as much butter to it as it will take – add in about 125g. If it becomes too buttery, balance it out by adding shuyo dashi.

Assembly. Put the porridge on the plate and make a small well in the centre. Add in a tbsp of medlar jelly. Put the sliced reindeer over. When we serve it, we put a couple of bay leaves on top of the reindeer, set them alight and put a cloche over them. It creates a bit of theatre and also gives you that aroma that is reminiscent of a forest – or, the lonesome pine.

114

MOMO·NO·KI

The Bacon and the Egg

It is one of the great combinations. Bacon and egg has been around since time immemorial and people never grow tired of it. That doesn't mean it can't be reimagined for the 21st century. The flavours are those that we've all grown up with and still love – but the range of textures, the colour and the presentation give it a new lease of life.

SERVES 1

4 rashers MAPLE CURED BACON
65g BUTTER
1 EGG YOLK
½ tsp WHITE-WINE VINEGAR
Drop of ICE-COLD WATER
Squeeze of LEMON
SALT
OAK or HICKORY CHIPS

OPTIONAL EXTRAS

1 DUCK EGG
MICROHERBS AND FLOWERS

Start by making a basic hollandaise. Melt your butter and skim off any solids. Keep warm. Then add the egg yolk and white-wine vinegar, with a pinch of salt and a drop of ice cold water, in a metal bowl. Whisk vigorously. Now place the metal bowl over a pan of gently simmering water and whisk until it emulsifies. Remove from the heat and gently incorporate the butter, little by little, until it's creamy. If it becomes too thick, add water. Season with lemon. Now decant into a cup and smoke, by covering the top of the cup with clingfilm and running a smoke gun into it. Smoulder oak or hickory chips and stir through, while keeping covered with clingfilm.

Fry pieces of bacon until crisp. Now cover with maple syrup and allow to sit for three minutes under a moderate grill, ensuring it does not blacken. Chargrill your asparagus and spring onions and cut some of the stalks at 90 degrees, so that they stand upright.

If you want to add more egg, place half a 62C sous-vide duck egg on the plate.

Assembly. Make like Jackson Pollock and have some fun. Add the bacon, drizzle the hollandaise and garnish with microherbs and flowers.

MOMO·NO·KI

Angkor What?

SERVES 1

180g trimmed SIRLOIN BEEF
10g WASABI POWDER
50g fresh SPINACH LEAVES
PINCH OF SALT
5g HY FOAMER
5g XANTHAN GUM
Small handful of preserved KOMBU
3cm piece of CUCUMBER, cut into fine dice
2 ASPARAGUS SPEARS
Handful of ENOKI MUSHROOMS

I cook my sirloin in a vacpac bag, in a sous-vide machine, at 56.5C for 50 minutes. It gives the perfect result. My steak comes out of the vacpac and goes straight into iced water, so that it stops cooking and retains its glorious texture.

Home cooks are unlikely to be able to go down that route, so sear the steak in a hot pan for two minutes on either side, then give it five minutes in a 180C oven to finish. Vary the cooking times to suit your personal taste.

Now make your wasabi and spinach chlorophyll. Take the wasabi and spinach leaves and blitz in a food processor. Slowly add a drizzle of water, then your hy foamer and xanthan gum. You'll get a really clean foam, which you can set aside.

Now shred the reconstituted kombu and mix with the cucumber dice. Chargrill the asparagus spears and deep fry the enoki mushrooms for 90 seconds.

Assembly. If you have cooked your beef sous vide, you'll need to fry it off for two minutes on each side, add butter, then rest. Sit the beef on the spinach and wasabi chlorophyll, top it with the kombu and cucumber garnish and then dress the plate with asparagus and enoki mushrooms.

118

Piggie Smalls

This celebration of all things pork has rapidly become one of our best-selling dishes.
It's a deeply satisfying dish and our customers love it. It's amazing that so many
complementary flavours are available from two principal ingredients – pork and apples.

SERVES 1

1 MARMALADE SAUSAGE
2 × 3cm cubes of BACON from a whole side
1 IBERICO CHORIZO (sausage-sized)
MAPLE SYRUP, to drizzle
1 GREEN APPLE
2 SPRING ONIONS
4 ASPARAGUS SPEARS
RAPESEED OIL
APPLE POWDER (from MSK)
1 tbsp MEDLAR (or QUINCE or CRAB
   APPLE) JELLY
150g CONFIT BELLY PORK
APPLE-INFUSED VINAIGRETTE
25g MUSCAT SULTANAS

Take a 4cm × 4cm × 2cm piece of confit pork belly. Finish off in butter, in a hot pan, then pop it into a 170C oven for five minutes, to warm through. Drizzle maple syrup over your bacon, then pop it into a medium oven for 16–18 minutes. The sausage can be baked, fried or grilled until cooked through, along with the chorizo, which should be dressed with maple syrup and baked for about 12 minutes. You can add other elements to the dish; a cubed piece of loin with the crackling still on is delicious if it's available.

Now the apple: I take a green apple and slice rounds from it using a mandolin. I usually use about four on the plate. I also take two more rounds, remove the skin and cut into julienne. I also make an apple sauce and a green apple vinaigrette and finish the plate with apple dust, which we buy from a specialist supplier. Chargrill your asparagus and spring onions, after dressing in rapeseed oil.

Assembly. We place our apple rounds on the plate and use them as the base for a number of components. So, for instance, you can cut your sausages and chorizo lengthways, then at 90 degrees, so that they stand tall. Perch a piece of bacon against them, almost as though they are a tower, then drizzle with medlar jelly, or shroud in apple dust.

Make sure you reserve some of the crackling from your belly pork, so that you can add that to the plate. Finish with a few muscat sultanas, which you'll find at a deli or online.

The Corn Field

There's something deliciously soulful and satisfying about The Corn Field. It's comfort food, it's food that feels as though it puts its arm around you and gives you a big old hug. Big on flavour and bursting with colour, it's perfect at any time of day or night.

SERVES 1

1 CORN ON THE COB
1 SHALLOT, finely diced
100g CURED COUNTRY HAM
½ tbsp BLONDE MISO
Dash of FISH SAUCE
2 SPRING ONIONS, finely chopped
75ml DASHI
½ a 62-DEGREE DUCK EGG (p49), (or a
   SOFT POACHED EGG)

Boil a corn cob for about five minutes, until the pieces of corn turn from yellow to a golden colour. Remove, leave to cool, then take a knife and cut off all the kernels.

Pan-fry a shallot in a little oil or butter. Now cut the country ham into lardons and pan-fry with the shallots. Throw in your corn, and finish off for another minute or two. Add the blonde miso and stir in, while still frying.

Add a dash of fish sauce and throw in spring onions. The savoury ingredients will form a crust on the bottom of the pan, so add a little dashi to deglaze and release all of those wonderful flavours.

Assembly. Simply serve in a bowl, with a 62-degree duck egg, as shown.

The Stones

Shredded rib-eye beef, a hit of bulgogi sauce and delicious shiitake: this dish features many of the things that I love about Korean cooking. Great flavours, quick, vibrant and with explosive flavours; you can't beat it. It gets its name from the salt blocks on which we serve it – and because it's a rock'n'roll dish.

SERVES 4

500g RIB-EYE STEAK, shredded
300g JASMINE RICE
1 tsp FISH SAUCE
CHICKEN STOCK
SESAME OIL
BULGOGI SAUCE
1 EGG
4 tbsp KIMCHI
Generous handful of CUCUMBER ribbons
200g BEANSPROUTS
8 SPRING ONIONS, finely chopped
Generous handful of PICKLED SHIITAKE
Handful of PEANUTS
1 RED ONION, sliced
2 GARLIC CLOVES, puréed
FISH SAUCE, to season
½ BIRD'S-EYE CHILLI, finely chopped
1 tsp GOCHUJAN
CORIANDER

Heat the stone/block, so that it will help the dish to retain its heat when you serve it. If you're not serving it on saltblocks, remember to add a little extra bulgogi sauce. Salt blocks will have a residual salty flavour, so you don't need as much bulgogi if you're using one.

Make your rice, using water and chicken stock. Cook for 20 minutes, until tender. Stir through the coriander, fish sauce and chilli and allow to stand for 10 minutes.

To a smoking wok, add sesame oil and the red onion, shredded beef, spring onions, beansprouts and garlic. Stir fry for two minutes, until the meat is starting to cook. Now add the bulgogi sauce.

Assembly. Spoon the beef onto your salt blocks, or into a bowl, then add the cucumber ribbons, pickled shiitake, crushed peanuts and additional condiments. The gochujan will add heat, because it is made from red chilli, glutinous rice, soybeans and salt, which have been naturally fermented. Sprinkle liberally with coriander.

桃の木

MOMO·NO·KI

PASTRY

Rules of pastry

My golden rule for pastry is this: there are no rules.

Many cookbooks will tell you that you have to be accurate to the final gram when you're cooking desserts. There's a lot of truth in that. Pastry is a science and if you make a minor mistake, the results can be disastrous. Puddings might not rise, they might be too dense, they can split or they can be soggy.

That, however, obscures an even more important truth. When it comes to making desserts, throw the rulebook out of the window. For sure, make sure your measurements, temperatures and timings are accurate – but there are no other rules.

Take the example of Momo·No·Ki's signature puddings. All of them were created with a smile on our faces and a knowing smile. Take Momo•No•Ki's nest as an example: most recipe books will tell you to serve crème brûlée in glass ramekins, or similar vessels. But that's boring. And it doesn't tell the whole story. The eggs for our brûlées come from our own chickens – so we hollow out the eggshells, fill a basket with the same straw that the hens use for bedding and serve them like that. It tells a story, it puts a smile on our customers' faces and it's a bit of fun.

Um Bongo is similar. We love exotic fruit: passion fruit and mango explode delicious, subtropical flavours. When we were thinking of a way to marry some of those flavours we were inspired by a daft advertisement that used to appear on TV many years ago. We took the

idea and ran with it, creating a dessert that is light, flavoursome and really good fun.

Burt's Bassetts is another crowd pleaser. The inspiration for that is obvious – but, wow, what a dessert.

The point I'm trying to make is really quite simple. Yes, you have to create desserts following tried-and-tested recipes, whether you're making panna cotta, jelly, flapjack or crème brûlée. But those techniques should be a beginning, not an end. They should merely be tools at your disposal, rather than the finished product. Once you've mastered those methods, find new and creative ways of using them.

Think outside the box, do something different and have fun.

When it comes to pastry, the bottom line is this: let your imagination be your guide.

Toffee Crisp

This dish was inspired by one of my favourite chocolate bars. We didn't want to simply recreate it, we wanted to do something a little bit different. We created a dish that looks spectacular – we encase the dessert in 'maple glass' – and tastes absolutely delicious. A lot of our customers love this pudding, and so do we . . .

MAKES 1 LARGE TOFFEE CRISP
  CHEESECAKE – SERVES 12

BASE
200g CHOCOLATE DIGESTIVES
6 TOFFEE CRISPS
100g UNSALTED BUTTER

FILLING
6 TOFFEE CRISPS
550g MASCARPONE
550g SOFT CHEESE
100g MAPLE SYRUP

OPTIONAL EXTRAS
100g DARK SUGAR – for the filling
MAPLE GLASS – see below

Make your base by smashing the chocolate digestive biscuits and Toffee Crisps and adding to a large pan with the melted butter. Make sure that all of the chocolate, biscuit and melted butter are incorporated, so that you have a glossy mix. Use the back of a wooden spoon or spatula to press down on the mix and make sure there are no dry pieces of biscuit. Now fill a large baking tray, or tin, with the mix and refrigerate for at least an hour, until completely set.

Now make your filling. Fold the mascarpone and soft cheese together, then fold in the maple syrup and then add smashed Toffee Crisps. Check the mix, to see whether it's sweet enough for you. If you want a sweeter version, take 100g of dark sugar and blitz it in your food processor, so that it's the consistency of icing sugar. Gently fold in a little at a time, until it is the desired sweetness. Use a spatula to spoon onto the base, then return to the fridge to chill and set.

Optional extras. We serve our Toffee Crisps by cutting an oblong from the tray and encasing it in maple glass. The glass is made by making a caramel (see p138), using maple syrup. That is then poured onto a heatproof mat and left to set. You can either use a hot knife to cut through it, or you can make mini moulds for it, so that it sets into your desired shape.

130

The Island

The island is served with all manner of garnishes, including chocolate soil, fresh mint, viola flowers and delicious chocolate pebbles, not forgetting shards of pulled caramel.

SERVES 4
CARAMEL
90ml DOUBLE CREAM
28g BUTTER
24g HONEY
24ml WATER
80g CASTER SUGAR

CHOCOLATE NEMESIS
270g DARK CHOCOLATE
270g CASTER SUGAR
180g UNSALTED BUTTER
4 EGGS

GOOD-QUALITY VANILLA ICE-CREAM

Caramel. Heat the cream and butter, until they are fully incorporated. Now boil the honey, water and sugar, then add the cream mix. Boil for about 10 minutes to 120C. (See page 139 for caramel tips.)

Nemesis. Melt the chocolate and butter, then add the caramel to the chocolate mix. Whisk the eggs and sugar for 10 minutes, then fold the chocolate mix into the eggs. Put into a tray and bake at 120C for one hour.

Assembly. Place a ball of ice-cream in each bowl. Spoon caramel-chocolate nemesis over the top and then decorate with chocolate soil (there are various methods for making chocolate soil, the easiest of which is to take a packet of Minstrels and blitz them at a high speed in a food processor!), mint, edible flowers and other garnishes. You could also use fruit – strawberries work a treat.

Momo•No•Ki's Nest

When we take vast nests to the table, our customers wonder what to think. We serve our crème brûlée in hollowed-out eggshells. We carefully saw through the tops and remove them. Then we add shards of caramel and present it all in a 'nest' made from straw. It has a real 'wow' factor.

MAKES 4

SHORTBREAD
150g PLAIN FLOUR
1 EGG
50g BUTTER
100ml OLIVE OIL

CARAMEL
125g BUTTER
100g SOFT BROWN (or CASTER) SUGAR
1 can CONDENSED MILK

CHOCOLATE TOPPING
350g DARK CHOCOLATE
20g OF BUTTER

PISTACHIO CREME BRULEE
500ml DOUBLE CREAM
5 EGG YOLKS
75g SUGAR
1 VANILLA POD, split
60g PISTACHIO NUTS, blanched and peeled

Shortbread. Mix together the flour and softened butter, then adding the egg and the olive oil. Shape your mix into a circle and keep in the fridge for 25 minutes.

Caramel. Put your can of condensed milk into a pan with hot water and simmer gently for 30 minutes, to make a *dulce de leche*. Make sure there is always water in the pan – otherwise the can will explode. Melt the butter and milk in a pan and add the dulce de leche to that. Remove your shortbread from the fridge and put into a preheated 160C oven for around 30 minutes, until golden brown. When the shortbread and caramel are both cool, pour the caramel on top and refrigerate for two hours.

Chocolate topping. Melt the chocolate in a bain-marie and incorporate the butter. Pour over the caramel and refrigerate for a further 15 minutes. Cut into slices when cool and set.

Brûlée. Grind your pistachios in a pestle and mortar, if using. Separate the egg yolks and blend with the sugar. Set aside. Pour the double cream into a saucepan and simmer for five minutes, adding the pistachio paste (or compound). Pass through a fine tamis, if using paste, to make sure your brûlées are smooth. Return to the pan and add the vanilla pod, scraping all of the seeds into the mix. Add the cream and sugar, gently stirring. You're looking for a temperature around 88C. Pass through a sieve and then cool. Now blend at a high speed. Pour into your egg cups.

Burty's Bassetts

SERVES 12 (BUT SCALABLE)

LIQUORICE PANNA COTTA

1800ml DOUBLE CREAM

450ml MILK

18 sheets GELATINE

450g SUGAR

2 tbsp MSK LIQUORICE CONCENTRATE

2 tbsp BLACK FOOD COLOURING

COCONUT FONDANT ICING

450g PLAIN MARSHMALLOWS

700g ICING SUGAR

200g DESICCATED COCONUT

1½ tbsp WATER

BUTTER or MARGARINE, for greasing

LIQUORICE

225g BUTTER

350g SUGAR

395g TIN OF SWEET CONDENSED MILK

440g CORN SYRUP

1½ tbsp MSK LIQUORICE CONCENTRATE

2 tbsp BLACK FOOD COLORING

JELLY TOTS

135g FRUIT-FLAVOURED JELLY CUBES

3 tbsp WATER

Tube of HUNDREDS-AND-THOUSANDS
  SPRINKLES

We like to stay on our toes and make sure the customers' leave with smiles on their faces. These do the trick.

Panna cotta. Warm the double cream and milk, mix in the MSK liquorice concentrate, black food coloring and sugar. Soften the gelentine sheets in cool water then add to the mix, pour into moulds set in the fridge for two hours.

Now make the liquorice sweets – these are spears of liquorice wrapped in coconut fondant icing. To make the fondant icing, place the marshmallows in a microwave-safe bowl and set microwave on high setting for 30 seconds. Add the water. Grease a large spoon with butter or margarine, stir the marshmallows and keep melting in 30-second intervals until the marshmallows are smooth. Begin adding icing sugar and desiccated coconut, about 250g at a time, stirring between each addition, until the whole 900g is incorporated. At this stage the mixture gets sticky, so grease your hands with butter or margarine and knead on a greased work surface until smooth and no longer sticky.

To make the liquorice, place all the ingredients in a pan on a medium/high heat. Using a sugar thermometer heat to 110C. Pour into a lined tray. Cool for 30 minutes, then place into the fridge for six hours.

Roll out the coconut fondant icing and liquorice, using extra desiccated coconut if the mixture gets sticky. Shape as desired.

To make jelly tots, place the jelly and water in a microwave-safe bowl and set microwave on high setting for 30 seconds. Stir the jelly and keep melting in 30-second intervals until jelly has fully melted. Pour into moulds, set in fridge for an hour, then roll in the hundreds-and-thousands sprinkles.

SERVES 6
GUAVA JELLY
1 kg firm, ripe GUAVA
2 ltrs WATER
SUGAR (see method for quantity)
250ml GUAVA JUICE
2 LIMES, Freshly squeezed juice and
  grated zest of both
UM BONGO PANNA COTTA
12 ripe and wrinkly PASSION FRUITS
300ml DOUBLE CREAM
160ml MANGO PUREE
140g CASTER SUGAR
Juice of ½ A LEMON
12g sachet POWDERED GELATINE
2 tbsp ICING SUGAR
GUAVA JELLY
RASPBERRY COULIS for colour
COCONUT FLAPJACKS
125g BUTTER
2–3 tbsp GOLDEN SYRUP
90g ROLLED OATS
220g DARK BROWN SOFT SUGAR
85g DESICCATED COCONUT
155g PLAIN FLOUR
1½ tsp BAKING POWDER

Um Bongo

Way down deep in the middle of the Congo, a hippo took an apricot, a guava and a mango. He stuck it with the others, and he danced a dainty tango. The rhino said, "I know, we'll call it Um Bongo". Um Bongo, Um Bongo, They drink it in the Congo. And now they eat it at Momo•No•Ki. We had fun making this one. You'll have fun eating it.

Guava jelly. Wash the guava thoroughly, remove the stem then halve the fruit before placing in a large pan. Cover with the water then bring to a boil, cover and boil gently for 30 minutes. Use a spoon to pulp the fruit then strain through a large sieve. Pour the juice into a measuring jug and for every 250ml of liquid add 200g sugar. Add the lime zest and lime juice then return the mixture to the heat and bring to a vigourous boil. Continue cooking, stirring occasionally, until small bubbles begin to appear on the surface of the liquid. Measure for the setting point by placing a plate in the fridge. Spoon a little of the jelly onto the plate and when it forms a skin as you push it with your finger or the back of a spoon the gelling point has been reached. Allow to cool then pour into clean, sterilised jars. Seal, label and store until needed.

Panna cotta. Halve six of the passion fruit and scoop out the pulp into a saucepan. Add the cream, mango purée, caster sugar and lemon juice. Heat everything together, then gently boil, stirring until the sugar has dissolved. When the cream is just simmering, scoop out about 100ml into a small bowl and scatter over the gelatine. Stir until dissolved, stir back into the saucepan, then take off the heat. Press through a sieve into a jug, then pour the mixture into six sealable MSK

glass jars that have been lined with guava jelly. Also swirl some of the jelly through. Leave to set in the fridge for at least four hours until completely set.

Meanwhile, halve and scoop the rest of the passion fruit through a sieve into a bowl. Mix to sweeten with the icing sugar, add a tbsp of the seeds from the sieve back into the sauce, then stir to mix. This can be made up to two days in advance and chilled.

Flapjacks. Preheat the oven to 180C. Line an 18cm × 28cm tin with baking parchment. Melt butter in a pan with the golden syrup and stir until combined. In a large bowl sift together the flour and baking powder, then add brown sugar, oats and coconut. Add butter mixture to dry ingredients, and mix well. Press firmly into the prepared tin using the back of a spoon or the bottom of a glass. Place in the oven and bake for 20–25 minutes; the top should be slightly golden. Cool in tin, and cut into slices.

Assembly. To serve, top with raspberry coulis, slice of guava, half a passion fruit, and coconut flapjacks. Serve as shown.

Garnishes

We like our food to look pretty. And that means we pay attention to detail. Not all of you will dash out to the shops to buy red amaranth and you might not find yourselves making maple glass any time soon.

But I'd encourage you to have a go at simple sugar work. Making caramel, waiting for it to cool, then twisting it into all manner of shapes – like molten, blown glass – is remarkably rewarding.

And, best of all, it's simple.

One of the golden rules is to make sure that all of your equipment is clean. If there are any impurities, in either your ingredients or your cooking equipment, they will affect the end result.

Making caramel is easy and there are two basic types: wet and dry.

A dry caramel is made by heating sugar until it melts. Wet caramel uses water and sugar. It cooks more slowly but is less likely to burn. However, wet caramel can sometimes be prone to problems caused by crystallisation.

Take a safety-first approach. Molten sugar is seriously hot and can cause nasty burns. Caramel can reach temperatures of 170C, so please be careful, and make sure you do not let it come into contact with your skin.

To make dry caramel, simply take a non-stick frying pan, add your sugar and then place it on a medium heat. Continue to stir, so that it cooks evenly. You want to avoid a situation where sugar in the parts of the pan that are hottest burn, while others have yet to melt.

Remember, the darker the colour, the more bitter the flavour. You're looking for a honey-gold colour, to be on the safe side.

When it reaches the desired colour, pour quickly onto a non-stick mat. Wait for a minute or so until it starts to solidify. Then, taking tweezers, gently prise the ends and start to stretch it out. The ends will cool more quickly, so the centre will be pliable and easy to stretch. Pull, twist and tease into long shards. When you're pleased with the results, put on a cooling rack, to solidify.

If there's been one over-riding inspiration for Momo No Ki, it's the continent that gave us our name.

I love Asia. I am an unashamed Asia-phile. I love the people and the food; the flavours and the philosophies. I love the countryside and the attitude; the history and the heritage.

I've spent plenty of time travelling through Asia, enjoying different tastes, textures and smells. My passion for it is shared by my wife, Jo. I took her to Thailand and she was hooked.

Asian food has always been full of crackerjack flavours. It's like nothing else on earth.

You can travel to other parts of the world, to North America, South America, Africa, Europe or Australia, and find similarities with other places. Yan almost join the dots and work out why a place evolved in a particular way. You can usually trace the origins of the food, and work out that things originated in France, Spain, Italy and so on. You can't do that with Asia, it is utterly unique.

I've always found lifestyles a lot more laid back in Asia than they are in Europe. The freedoms that exist in Asia don't quite exist in Europe. The Western world can sometimes feel quite stoic, maybe even a little dull.

But Asia always feels full of energy. It pulses with life. It's a rock'n'roll continent.

I've enjoyed some crazy times in Asia. There have been episodes where I've been stuck in border gambling towns, like Poipet, in Cambodia, which is an insane place. I've known I've needed to get out, but something has drawn me back. There's a phrase that Asian travellers use when they've walked on the wild side, which is: 'You've gone a bit bamboo.' And there have been times when that's happened to me. But such experiences are life-affirming. They're part of what makes us human.

Asia is changing at an alarmingly fast rate. I remember travelling to Vietnam when it was first opened up. Back then, it was a real OMG place. It was the craziest place on earth. There were times when I'd find myself walking through streets that I shouldn't have been on. The danger would give me a thrill. I'd know I shouldn't be there, but I wouldn't be able to help myself. My wanderlust has taken me to full-moon parties, which used to be completely wild.

These days, its different. Parts of Asia now seem somehow tamer

YAMAGOYA RAMEN
山小屋拉面

than they used to be. The world is becoming increasingly westernised and the freedoms and adventures that travellers once enjoyed are disappearing fast. The food, however, remains just as cutting edge.

My first trip to Asia was with a friend, who was also a chef. I've always had an adventurous palate, which I inherited from my mother when she worked in kitchens in Africa. I would eat whatever was put before me. My friend, however, didn't want to eat ethnic food and would routinely order whatever English dishes he could find. But eventually he was forced out of his comfort zone and had to try different dishes. He was unbelievably happy that he did.

I love the balance of flavours in Asian cooking. There is a complicated mix of sweet and sour, salt and sugar, bitter and umami. It's proper knock-you-out stuff. And it's everywhere. In Thailand, you can buy a portion of pad thai for 15 bhat, or 30p, which is absolutely sensational. I don't imagine people from Thailand are as complimentary when they come to Britain and try a bag of chips.

I've eaten at some of the best restaurants in south-east Asia and memories of great dishes are strong in my mind.

"There's a phrase that Asian travellers use when they've walked on the wild side, which is: 'You've gone a bit bamboo.' Such experiences are life-affirming. They're part of what makes us human."

At the Mango Rooms, in Hoi An, Vietnam, I ate the most incredible prawns. They were cooked so simply it was ridiculous. They'd been smeared with an Indochine paste that was like an explosion of flavour.

142

桃の木

Another restaurant that blew me away was Cha Ca Thang Long, in Hanoi, in Vietnam. All they serve is cha ca, which is fish grilled at the table, with rice noodles and a fermented dipping sauce. It is incredible, it's really out of this world. I tried to recreate that dish for years and years but eventually realised that I would never manage to.

Travelling through Asia is a voyage of discovery. Wherever I go, I try to cook. I also make sure I visit the local markets and buy whatever new foods I find. It's always fun to play around with foods that I've not eaten before and try different types of seasonings.

One of the biggest lessons I've learned is that it takes time to truly understand Asian food. The bitter, salt, sweet, sour, umami are so different to what we do in the West. Those seasonings come from experience. They are something that you learn. If you gave the same Asian recipe to ten different chefs, they would each cook it differently.

This book, then, is simply a guide. It's a culinary tour around some of my favourite destinations. You should adapt it to your own tastes; adding more of this or less of that, to suit your own palate. Strap yourself in and enjoy the ride.

MOMO·NO·KI

Food with a heart

There's more to food than fun and good times.

It's important to put something back into the communities that inspire our dishes.

So Jo and I took a week out of our two-week holiday to Northern Thailand, to spend time working with Daughters Rising. Following that, we didn't want to return home. It was an eye-opening, life-affirming experience and we felt very humbled by it.

Daughters Rising works to empower at-risk girls who are vulnerable to sex-traffickers. It works to end sex-trafficking and exploitation by communities, as well as breaking the cycle of inter-generational poverty.

It tackles serious issues.

As many as two million children are forced into prostitution every year and more than half of them live in Asia. Unlike a lot of problems in developing countries, the problem of sex-trafficking is actually getting worse. At the peak of the Transatlantic slave trade, 80,000 slaves were transported from Africa to the new world. Today, more than 10 times as many women are being forced into brothels or other forms of slavery.

Every 30 seconds, another person becomes a victim.

Women are lured by traffickers with false promises of low-skilled jobs such as domestic help, models, and other jobs, and are then forced to work as prostitutes. But Daughters Rising teaches us that our generation can end this horrible human-rights violation, and everyone has a role.

It's so important to shut down the perpetrators and save girls, but it's also important to prevent it from happening to girls at all. Daughters Rising believes that offering incentives for educating a girl will make its less likely for parents to sell their daughter into prostitution. It believes that teaching a girl about confidence, women's rights and health can empower her against traffickers. It believes that with access to education women can pursue their dreams.

When we stayed with the charity, we realised that no barriers were insurmountable. Though Jo and I didn't have the language skills required to strike up a conversation, we found we were still able to communicate.

桃の木

"Daughters Rising believes
that teaching a girl a skill

pursue their dreams."

Food was our shared language. As a professional chef, I spent a lot of my time with Burmese refugees who were the victims of horrific abuse. They had been treated in the most appalling way but were finding ways to rebuild their lives. They were inspirational people and we did what we could to help them.

I spent time cooking with some of the women, showing them new techniques so that they would have skills that would enable them to get jobs in kitchens. It's really important for those girls to develop skills, so that they can escape the cycle of abuse. Those who work and earn a wage are less vulnerable to the predatory intentions of sex-traffickers. They move out of harm's reach.

During the course of our week with the charity, we tried to build confidence, as well as skills. The results were remarkable. As the days passed, the women realised they could trust us. They understood that we didn't want to take anything from them, or harm them in any way. They realised that we were their friends, that we were on their side.

Daughters Rising is not just involved in providing cooking workshops. It also provides education across a number of different fronts. It created RISE workshops to teach real-world computer skills, confidence, women's rights and health in a supportive peer-driven environment.

The workshops are in locations defined by the UN as points of origin, transit and destination for persons trafficked for sexual exploitation. The workshops are completely free, and help Daughters Rising to

identify candidates for scholarships. RISE workshops give families hope for a better future that starts with staying in school and results in more earning power and changing the fabric of their community.

The charity also launched the RISE UP shop in 2011, to help mothers in impoverished rural villages to earn for their families. It buys handmade crafts at a fair price to sell online to a larger western audience and then invests 100 per cent of the proceeds back into the next generation of young women. The charity connects and facilitates collaborations between indigenous craftswomen and artisans with designers to create unique jewellery and accessories. It is working towards developing sustainable models and increasing distribution.

As well as taking direct action, Daughters Rising is also raising awareness — and I hope that by writing a little bit about their work in Momo No Ki, I can play a small part in providing you with information.

It is currently developing projects and events to raise awareness and advocacy. It believes that by using the same tactics found in advertising, or the same story-telling techniques in screenwriting, or the same emotional engagement in games — it will be able to reach and

affect people in profound ways. It is meeting with artists, designers, copywriters, screenwriters, directors, animators, musicians and developers to create outstanding projects.

The people who run the organisation are truly remarkable. Alexa Pham, the programme director, inspired us with her passion for humanitarian work, which has propelled her on an adventure throughout the world for the past decade working with nonprofit-making organisations from Germany to Nepal. She spearheads the grant writing, fundraising, developing RISE workshops and other programs. She is part of an incredible team whose work makes a difference to improve the lives of some of the most vulnerable and needy people in the world. Sharing six pages of my book to tell you about their story is my small way of helping.

I commend them to you and if you're interested in contributing, or learning more, please contact Daughters Rising at info@daughtersrising.org or by visiting **www.daughtersrising.org**

There are other remarkable organisations doing great work in Thailand and one of them is Chai Lai Orchid, which has nature bungalows on the outskirts of Chiang Mai, in the northern mountains of Thailand.

Nestled within the untamed, bamboo forest sits a one-of-a-kind eco resort, the Chai Lai Orchid.

The property is also home to an elephant camp and visitors can spend their days caring and interacting with elephants; feeding, bathing, and playing with them. There are Thai cooking classes and picnics in the forest, as well as fresh fruit right from the tree. The family-style, cozy eco-bungalows provide the perfect space in which to escape to nature and experience the harmony of the mountain spirit. Details are at **www.chailaiorchid.com**

MOMO·NO·KI

The Peach Tree

Dedication, teamwork and inspiration are among the ingredients that have made The Peach Tree Shrewsbury's most successful restaurant.

Throw in a dash of inspiration, a liberal seasoning of talent and you have a combination that makes us tick.

We've never forgotten our roots – our exceptional relationships with local suppliers means we deliver farm-to-fork flavours that follow the seasons. If it's seasonal, flavoursome and in abundance, we'll find a knockout dish and put it on the menu.

The Peach Tree appeals to a broad church. We have a guy in the kitchen who is fanatical about sandwiches and makes the best in town. We have another guy who is in love with puddings: we asked him to make a Liquorice-Allsorts-inspired dessert and the results were astounding.

Tom, our group sous chef, and Rob, our group senior sous chef, have terrific experience and deliver the goods when the going gets tough. The heat of a busy kitchen brings out the best in both of them.

It's not just about the kitchen, of course, and we're proud of our front-of-house team. They provide friendly, informal service and go the extra mile to make people feel welcome and valued.

The Peach Tree is a restaurant for everybody. Great coffee and sensational macaroons, light lunches and fine dining – it all features on our day-round menu.

Of course, you wouldn't expect us to rest on our laurels. While we pay homage to the tried and trusted classics, we continue to push the boundaries.

During our years in Abbey Foregate, we've explored a variety of cuisines from around the globe. Fragrant and aromatic Middle Eastern food has proved popular and we're looking forward to revising that part of the world in future menus. We're also turned on by the dishes emerging from South America. From spiced beef empanadas to satisfying ceviche, from lomo saltado to quinoa salad with mint and mango, and from barbecued sirloin with chimichurri sauce to cassava and cheese fritters, we'll be staying at the cutting edge by serving food from around the world.

We're also planning to turn our attentions on foods that are closer to home. Foraging has become increasingly popular in recent years and we're looking to work with experts who know where to find the best natural foods in surrounding woods and countryside.

The Peach Tree remains a hub of culinary creativity with a redoubtable team. Wherever our tastebuds take us – from Mexico to Morocco, from Turkey to Tanzania – you can be sure we'll leave no stone unturned in our quest to bring you the brightest and best flavours from around the world.

The journey so far . . .

It started in West Africa, of all places. That's where I spent a happy, carefree childhood, growing up in the secure, loving environment provided by my mother and father, Valerie and Chris. My Dad was a diamond miner, stationed in Sierra Leone, and Mum ran a restaurant for expats. I owe my love of food to her.

Mum's restaurant was called The Club House and it seated 400 people. It was situated on a golf club and she would spend long hours cooking each day. Her customers were always well-fed and happy.

I spent most of my time in her kitchen, being looked after by my nanny, Helen, while Mum cooked. The experience gave me only happy memories of food.

Mum in Africa

Food became my first love. It evokes the fondest of memories, and transports me back to happier times.

Our time in Sierra Leone was relatively short. There was a military coup and Dad was arrested and thrown into prison. We eventually secured his release and fled. I remember Mum coming into my room in the middle of the night, grabbing me, and boarding us on an aeroplane back to England. We never went back.

I came from a hard-working family. When we returned to Britain, Dad got a job working for British Coal – just as the miners' strike took hold.

Food continued to play an important role in my life. We spent a lot of time staying with my Grandma, Dorothy, who farmed 150 acres outside Huddersfield. We'd do the milking and run errands on the farm; it was truly idyllic. She'd cook on a massive range and then we'd go shooting or fishing, bagging food for supper.

Dorothy lived with her brother, Robert, who played a huge role in my life. He was one of my biggest influences. He was a true Yorkshireman: a hard-worker who was careful with his money. He'd set me tasks, encouraging me to do chores such as fetching logs. He'd pay me a few bob. He instilled a work ethic, which I've never lost. Those days were halcyon: I'd cook at the stove with Mum and Dorothy – it was only natural that I became a chef.

Once I left school, I followed the herd. I went to catering college and worked in local restaurants in Huddersfield. I was always keen to better myself, to work hard and be the best that I could be. I landed a job at The Savoy, in London, and then moved on to Le Manoir aux Quat'Saisons. Kitchens were tough back in the 1980s and we got a rollocking every day, for one thing or another, but they were inspirational times. I was surrounded by great chefs and learned a great deal.

My first head chef's job was in Shropshire, at Rowton Castle, and I stayed on for a couple of years before taking a break and travelling the world. I return to Rowton refreshed and then moved to the Four Crosses at Bicton, as head chef for Jeff Blundell. My wanderlust took me back off around the world three or four years later and I spent a lot of time in south-east Asia. It really connected: I went to Thailand, Malaysia and Indonesia and fell in love with those places, forming a particularly strong bond with Bali.

I loved the food, the philosophy and the way of life. I'd developed a keen interest in Buddhism prior to my travels and my experiences cemented my beliefs. Buddhists like to stay calm; they are interested in being better people and in trying to help others. Travelling to south-east Asia didn't turn me into a Buddhist – it made me realise I already was one. That faith helps me enormously when I'm in the kitchen. When we've got 200 orders to deliver, you have to have something to fall back on.

I climbed, surfed and travelled during my time in Indonesia before receiving a call from The Peach Tree. They urgently needed a head chef and asked me to come home. It was 1998 and the rest is history.

I met my wife, Jo, not long after starting at The Peach Tree. Within a couple of months I'd flown off to Thailand. When I got home, Jo had moved in, we were married not long after, and we'll be together until the end.

Wedding day, 2002

Back in those days The Peach Tree was small. Two of us did everything: the prep, the cooking and even the washing up. We did 30 covers and worked our socks off.

Over time, we transformed the place. Our food then was quite rustic: steaks, chicken with morels, a truckle of woodland mushrooms – that sort of thing. How things have changed. Today, we cook food from around the world. We follow our hearts. We trust our instincts.

As a chef, there comes a point when confidence and ability overtake the impulse to 'do the right thing'. You no longer worry about other people's expectations of you. You start to create fashions, rather than follow them. You innovate and create. You become brave enough to have the courage of your convictions. You start to lead from the front.

My travels through Asia have had a profound effect on my food. We were serving Pad Thai 13 years ago, when nobody else knew what it was. We served Malaysian and Indonesian food, when nobody else was doing that.

The Peach Tree has been a constant progression. We've learned why flavours work together, we've assimilated an Asian mentality, almost, and have an intuitive understanding of combinations. We marry ingredients harmoniously. We treat dishes with respect.

Of course, we put a very British twist on our dishes. Da Umami Bomb, for instance, is served with kale and asparagus, rather than Asian greens. And why wouldn't it be? British greens are fantastic and they work beautifully in that dish.

During my years at the Peach Tree I've amassed a terrific amount of knowledge. I've decoded and deciphered dishes from around the world. I've learned techniques that add a 1 per cent difference to the flavour of a dish. I'm proud to present a selection of my favourites here. I sincerely hope you enjoy eating them.

Index of primary ingredients

Thanks . . .

my long suffering shabadoo, dad, my dear old mum for putting the fire in my belly, sidartha, martin monahan a true friend, paul monahan, strenk, pazzer, tom 'oddbod' garstone, robbie simmons, the sexy sam 'aubrey' butler, despicable jay, the hen, mark & misako i couldn't have done this without your vision, suree a true lady, mr & mrs teague, krispy squint the keogh, bimberly, stiffler, brenda bevan, mardis gras micheal, johnny "honourib' stone", omar 'A Salam a Lakum' bojang, my little zoe beercan, orange, the brain, adamo, tinsly the 'C&^%t', aggy, gascuat, abi ballz, james 'the love rat' eweings, andy richardson & adam the design guru, kev kardashian, my little willy . . .

you're all legendz

AND MY SUPPLIERS:

Setonaikai, 25 The Parade, St Mary's Place, Shrewsbury SY1 1DL
www.setonaikai.co.uk

MSK Specialist Ingredients, Kurzon House, Main Road Ind Est, Unstone, Dronfield S18 4AB
www.msk-ingredients.com

Rowlands Fresh Produce Ltd, Knights Way, Battlefield Enterprise Park, Shrewsbury SY1 3AB
www.rowlandsltd.co.uk

Great Ness Oil Ltd, The Old Parsonage, Little Ness, Shrewsbury SY4 2LG
www.greatnessoil.co.uk

Lakeside Meats, Unit 1, Dorrington Business Park, Dorrington, Shrewsbury SY5 7JP

Appleyards Deli, 85 Wyle Cop, Town Centre, Shrewsbury SY1 1UT

Barkworths Seafoods, Stalls 16–17, Market Hall, Shrewsbury SY1 1HQ
www.barkworths.co.uk

Maynards Farm, Weston-under-Redcastle, Shrewsbury SY4 5LR
www.maynardsfarm.co.uk

Shrewsbury Bakehouse, 7 Castle Gates, Shrewsbury SY1 2AE
www.shrewsburybreads.co.uk

All the best!!.

Best of luck
& Good Cooking
matt xx

KEEP Cooking
AND Have fun
x